A
HISTORY
OF THE
CONTEMPORARY
JEWS

Solomon Grayzel

A
HISTORY
OF THE
CONTEMPORARY
JEWS

from 1900 to the present

A TEMPLE BOOK

ATHENEUM, NEW YORK, 1975

Published by Atheneum
Reprinted by arrangement with
The Jewish Publication Society of America
Copyright © 1960 by
The Jewish Publication Society of America
All rights reserved
Library of Congress catalog card number 60-15542
ISBN 0-689-70080-6
Manufactured in the United States of America by
The Murray Printing Company,
Forge Village, Massachusetts
Published in Canada by McClelland and Stewart Ltd.
First Atheneum Printing August 1969
Second Printing March 1972
Third Printing January 1975

Contents

IV

TWO DECADES OF RETROGRESSION

V

THE ORDEAL OF CIVILIZATION

VI

THE DIASPORA AFTER WORLD WAR II

VII

THE BALANCE SHEET OF A GENERATION

Acknowledgments

In 1956, Monde Publishers invited me to contribute a historical essay to a volume subsequently published under the title *Two Generations in Perspective*. The essay has been expanded and revised for purposes of this book. To make this review of the recent past more useful to students and to other readers not content with a rapid general survey, a brief bibliography and an index have been added.

I take pride and pleasure in listing the names of the friends who, having read the original essay, were kind enough to offer advice and make suggestions. I list their names, not in order to place upon them the slightest blame for any mistakes of fact or judgment that may be found in this book, but in order to thank them for their guidance. The distinguished scholars and men of letters to whom I owe this debt of gratitude are: Dr. Selig Adler, Dr. Bernard J. Bamberger, Arthur A. Cohen, Dr. M. J. Cohen, Dr. Moshe Davis, David J. Galter, Rabbi Philip Goodman, Dr. Oscar I. Janowsky, Dr. Guido Kisch, Dr. Bertram W. Korn, Rabbi Isidore S. Meyer, Dr. Jacob R. Marcus, Dr. Harry M. Orlinsky, Harry Schneiderman, Dr. Ephraim A. Speiser, Dr. Bernard D. Weinryb, Maxwell Whiteman, and Edwin Wolf, 2nd. These good men could no doubt have used their time and energy in a better cause, but not in behalf of a more grateful author.

SOLOMON GRAYZEL

June 1960

Foreword

One generation passeth away,
and another generation cometh;
And the earth abideth forever.
(Eccl. I:4)

In the moving message of farewell that Moses, greatest of the prophets, spoke to his people at the very beginning of their march through the centuries, he pleaded with them to study their history.

Remember the days of old;
Consider the years of many generations.
Ask your father and he will inform you,
Your grandfather and he will declare unto you . . .

Nowhere has the dependence of the Jews upon their past been more eloquently urged.

Few generations of Jews have lived through such crises

as has ours and that of our immediate predecessors. Few have had to make such basic decisions or to carry so much responsibility for all that Jews have held dear as have the Jews of the present day—the very ones for whom this book is intended. There has rarely been an age in greater need of the self-knowledge and the strength that can be derived from testing its own experience against the long and varied history of the Jewish people. Can we evaluate ourselves and our actions and so make sure that the Jewish heritage has not suffered at our hands and will be transmitted whole to our successors?

A generation cannot sit in judgment on itself. Its successors may reverse or even laugh at its values and standards, as we smile at the values and standards of some generations that have preceded us. What is even more important, no generation can tell how well it is preparing, or how badly it is neglecting, such powers as its successors will need to meet the challenges that they may have to face. Not knowing what these challenges will be, especially in an age of rapid change, how can a preceding generation prepare for them? Yet it is on the basis of such a sense of adequacy or inadequacy on its own part that the future will judge us. If it is hazardous to write the history of an age long past, it is presumptuous to try to point out the rights and wrongs, the good and evil, the encouraging and the distressing in the period through which one has lived and is living, and to measure the success of one's own generation in making it possible for some future generation to live Jewishly on the highest possible level.

But it is tempting. The past sixty years have not been merely turbulent; they have also been exceedingly interesting. We have witnessed vast changes in economics, society, and politics, great advances in science and technology, revolutions in the minds of men. The world has been in ferment. Inevitably, therefore, the ferment has been transmitted to the Jewish people as well. The Jews have always lived in the very center of world events, so that their experiences in any period have reflected the state of the human spirit. But is that all? Have our contemporary experiences been no more than reflections of a dynamic era? Has there been—to use a phrase made popular by a modern historian—no creative response to the challenges we have encountered? Have not the Jews drawn upon their accumulated spiritual resources and given a characteristic, distinctive turn to events? An appraisal of the events of the crowded decades just past seems to permit an affirmative answer. Our age has done what it could in the face of innumerable problems, tragedies, and opportunities. We have, within the limitations of human foresight, and sometimes purely Providentially, helped safeguard the future of the Jew and his heritage.

Because the United States is the home of the writer and of most of the prospective readers of this book, it is natural that in discussing Jewish experience during the generation or two just past, our center of attention should be the American Jewish community. Besides, United States Jewry now represents the world's largest and the foremost diaspora community. The successes and failures of this community must in the end count for more than similar successes and failures in smaller communities. Other communities, especially that of Israel, offer us opportunities for contrast and comparison and serve to illustrate the variety of Jewish attitudes toward problems and events.

Nevertheless, our chief interest remains the Jewish people, the entire people, whether in Israel or in the diaspora. For it is our belief, borne out by the millennial history of the Jews, that we are indivisible, that what happens to any one segment of the Jewish people affects every other. Our religion, our historical experience, and our sense of destiny bind us together. The ancient assertion, "All Israelites are responsible for one another," is but the diffuse and partial echo of that greater and humanly more inclusive cry: "Hear, O Israel, the Lord is our God; the Lord is one."

I

· ·

The New Diaspora

· ·

1. AS THE NEW CENTURY OPENED

Henrietta Szold, commenting on the closing year of the nineteenth century, remarked in the *American Jewish Year Book* (II) that the Jews were parting with that year, and that century, with no regrets. The strides made by anti-Semitism in the second half of the nineteenth century had belied the hopes and ideals its first half had produced. In the next *Year Book* (III), the first year of the twentieth century was described as having been marked in outstanding fashion by the work of the ICA (the Jewish Colonization Association) and by the appearance of the initial volume of *The Jewish Encyclopedia*. The work of the ICA was acclaimed as "bearing within itself the possibility of far-reaching influence upon the future of the Jewish People as long as the world may endure." The *Encyclopedia* was hailed as the product of great scholarship, and a sign of the awakening cultural interest of the American Jew. Events were to prove the writer overoptimistic on every count. The twentieth century was to outdo the nineteenth in anti-Semitism. Agricultural colonization was, indeed, to have far-reaching influence; but in Palestine rather than in the lands of the diaspora. *The Jewish Encyclopedia* proved to be an important work; but infinitely much more labor would have to be undertaken to arouse any considerable interest among the Jews in their cultural heritage.

There is no occasion for surprise at the optimism which pervaded these analyses of the Jewish situation at the turn of the century. The whole western world was then aglow with firm faith in uninterrupted progress; optimism was a natural concomitant. No one but a few prophets of doom foresaw the wars and revolutions, the fall of empires, the rise of savagery, that were to afflict the world within a few short decades. The forces that were to transform the world were already in motion, but few recognized them and fewer still did anything to forestall them. No one can be blamed for not being prophetic. It is nevertheless remarkable that perspicacious people like the editors of the *Year Book* failed to note the relative importance and the likely consequences of the movements that were to cause a transformation in Jewish life. They did note the vast migration from eastern Europe; but even so they did not appreciate what it would mean to the religion and culture of the American Jewish community, nor did they foresee the changes about to take place in other parts of the world.

2. THE EXODUS FROM EASTERN EUROPE

The seeds of the revolutionary changes Jewish life was to experience in the next half-century had already been sown. The great exodus from eastern Europe had already begun, and out of it was to stem most of what was destined to happen, in terms of both destructiveness and creativity, in the next two generations. Its beginnings must therefore be described.

Russia and Rumania were the chief culprits. The latter had repeatedly promised to grant its Jews equality of treatment, but was using every subterfuge to avoid doing so. The western nations looked on with some disdain, but did nothing to enforce the promises made at the Congress of Berlin in 1878. Only the United States openly showed its displeasure, though the practical effects of this attitude were nil. At the same time, the Russian government for its part openly proclaimed its intention of eliminating Russia's Jewish population. It embarked upon systematic persecution with whatever efficiency the czarist government was able to exercise. The pogroms in 1881 and 1882—actually encouraged by the authorities in various parts of the country—and the May Laws of the latter year, which drove the Jews from many towns and villages, left some dead, many homeless, and all of the Jews terrified. Thousands fled across the borders into Germany and Austria. They had only the vaguest idea of where they were going, and they certainly did not have the means of getting there. For the first time, the Jews of western Europe and America were faced with a vast refugee problem.

It was a problem the western Jews would have to face almost continuously and in aggravated form from then on. The revolutionary rumblings in Russia and the dissatisfaction with their lot of the middle and lower classes in Rumania continued to necessitate diversionary tactics—as a substitute for an honest facing of their internal problems—by the governments of these countries. In the past, anti-Jewish policies had served other governments elsewhere. Charging a helpless minority with responsibility for all the evils from which the nation was suffering had worked before; it would work again. The rulers of Russia and Rumania considered this technique a cheap and clever way of retaining power.

While emphasizing, as is proper, the social and economic causes—such as the increase in Jewish population and the growth of a non-Jewish middle class—for the flight of the Jews from Russia and Rumania, it is easy to forget that the Russian and Rumanian Jews could have solved their problem by becoming Christians. A very few did. The vast majority, however, stayed home and continued as Jews to suffer the economic and social restrictions imposed on them, as well as frequent physical attacks. A small minority—small compared to the Jewish population of eastern Europe, but quite large in absolute numbers—preferred to face exile. The first question to be answered was, therefore, Whither? A country of expanding industrial capacity offered the best opportunity. Germany, France, England, and some of the smaller states of western Europe were, it is true, close at hand, but they were not known to the Jews of eastern Europe as lands of opportunity. The United States, on the other hand, while farther away, had already become famous both for its hospitality to immigrants and for the presumed ease with which one could attain a degree of economic independence. There were other places of settlement available to those seeking new homes: South Africa and, to a lesser extent, Australia were opening up to European immigration.

Wherever they went, most of the Jews expected to engage in industry and commerce.

Another outlook, however, had become current among the Jews of that age, both in western and in eastern Europe, namely, that the lack of a farming population among the Jewish people was a fault. For centuries the Jews had been excluded from agriculture; now the severance of the Jews from the soil was being turned into an accusation against them. They themselves accepted their economic situation as anomalous and sought ways of correcting it. One group, which called itself *Am Olam* (Eternal People), favored establishing Jewish agricultural settlements anywhere in the world. Members of another group, equally interested in farming, aimed their agricultural efforts toward the additional achievement of the emotional, national goal of reviving the soil of their fathers in the Holy Land.

A movement toward the attainment of this goal had been in existence ever since the early 1860's. Under the name *Hovevei Tsiyon* (Lovers of Zion), it had been the expression of a yearning rather than a plan. But the exigencies of the 1880's gave it a practical turn. The Lovers of Zion issued a call to action, and young people responded as members of a group named BILU (a made-up word consisting of the first letters of the apocopated sentence, Isaiah 2:5: "House of Jacob, come and let us go . . ."), which for a time stirred considerable enthusiasm. Its net results were small, for the revival of Palestine, then a rocky wasteland inhabited by a small and impoverished Arab population, was too difficult a task for the scanty resources, apart from idealism, that the devoted young Biluists brought with them.

Each of the possible new homelands reacted to the flood of immigration which touched its borders; by the year 1900 each had a policy of its own. In the early 1880's, the western Jews tried to stem the tide of Russian emigrants and then to regulate it by giving guidance and assistance. The German Jews, being geographically the closest, established a central committee to raise money for the support of the needy among the Russian Jewish refugees and to speed them on their way. Before long the German committee enlisted the co-operation of the Alliance Israélite Universelle, of the London Mansion House Committee, and of others. The European Jewish committees quickly agreed among themselves that the vast majority of the emigrants from Russia would have to settle in the United States. A considerable number of American Jews received this decision with no enthusiasm whatever. However, the more liberal-minded American Jews prevailed, and the delegate of the Hebrew Emigrant Aid Society sought only to make sure that those encouraged to go on to the United States were physically fit to become self-supporting.

For some years the various European Jewish committees functioned separately in their respective countries and jointly at the border stations outside Russia. Had the flow of emigration lasted a year, or two, or three, or shown some signs of letting up eventually, these committees would no doubt have carried on according to their plans. Unfortunately, the flow increased rather than diminished. The dam which they had tried to set up proved completely useless in view of the situation in Russia. It became clear that all the Jewish organizations could do was to offer elementary guidance, and protection en route; their finances were unequal to anything else. This was the situation in 1900. By then any attempt to direct emigrants to, or away from, any country had been given up. It had become clear, moreover, that the greatest number by far were looking to settlement in the United States.

Immigration from eastern Europe to the United States had been going on for a long time, but because no one kept statistics on the subject, the number of immigrants before 1880 can only be guessed. There is reason to believe that the 1870's brought 30,000 east European Jews to the United States. Such immigration rose to about 135,000 in the ninth decade of that century and to 280,000 in the final decade.

Before describing the fate of the immigrants in the United

States and how their presence affected the Jewish population already there, two forces bearing on the problem of the Jews' search for a home must be dealt with. One of them was hailed as providing a definite solution, but proved quite inadequate; the other was widely condemned as illusory, but proved to be of tremendous importance.

The first was the attempt by German-born Baron Maurice de Hirsch, industrialist and railroad builder, to ease and guide the settlement of the immigrants in their new homes. In the early 1890's, he established a large fund under which Jewish immigrants to the United States would receive vocational training and be provided with tools. Later, impressed by the argument that farming was the most desirable occupation for the Jewish emigrants from eastern Europe, he set up another fund, this time in the huge sum of $40,-000,000, for the settlement on farms in North and South America of such Jews as were willing to forgo city life. Primarily under the direction of European Jews, a new organization, the Jewish Colonization Association, better known by its abbreviated title ICA, was established.

Baron de Hirsch was undoubtedly a great and imaginative benefactor. Thousands of Russian and Rumanian Jews heeded his call and settled in the Western Hemisphere in scores of farming communities from Manitoba in Canada to the southern part of the Argentine Republic, as well as in South Africa and Australia. Some of these farmers succeeded and some did not; some, like those in southern New Jersey in the United States, remained on the land for a generation and some for two. But the Baron's dream of solving the problem of the aimless Jewish emigrants from eastern Europe was hardly realized to anything like the extent he had envisioned. His great wealth did not suffice to achieve his difficult goal, which was nothing less than the reversal of economic habits enforced through more than a thousand years. Emotional conviction, not merely logic, was needed to bring about so great a change. But this was not yet evident in the year 1900, and it is therefore not surprising that

American Jews considered the founding of the Jewish Agricultural Society that year a very hopeful sign.

3. THE ZIONIST HOPE

On August 29, 1897, three years before the end of the nineteenth century, a different project was initiated to find a home for the homeless Jews. That day, in Basle, Switzerland, Theodor Herzl opened the First World Zionist Congress. Herzl, the assimilated European Jew, had been touched by the tragedy of the flight from Russia. Like many others among his western contemporaries, he had attributed the uprooting of the Jews from their east European homes to the cultural backwardness of those lands. Suddenly, in the course of the Dreyfus affair, it dawned on him that, where the Jews were involved, western civilization also was not immune to prejudice and cruelty. There was only one thing for the Jews to do, namely, to establish themselves as a nation in a homeland of their own. Herzl did not know at first that his idea had a long history, that many Jews and some Christians had advocated it before him. It came to him with the force of a revelation, and he could not rest until he had written it down in the form of a pamphlet, *The Jewish State.* He tried to interest his friends, and then a number of wealthy and influential Jews, among them Baron Maurice de Hirsch and Baron Edmond de Rothschild. None of these took him seriously. But when, despairing of these presumably practical men, he turned to the masses, he found enthusiastic support everywhere, and especially among the Jews of eastern Europe. For the first time in more than seventeen centuries, since the days of Bar Kokhba, a congress of Jews met, at Herzl's call, in Basle, to plan national policy for the entire Jewish people. They set forth their aim as "Zionism"; and they formulated their policy in what came to be known as the Basle Program. Zionism pledged itself to work for the establishment of a publicly recognized home for the Jewish people.

The idea made astonishing progress, not so much in realization as in the enthusiastic support it evoked. It also elicited bitter opposition and even condemnation. Both the support and the opposition are interesting because both reveal the mind of the Jews at the close of the nineteenth century. The fact that the Zionist aim was achieved only through a chain of circumstances impossible to foresee at that time seems to indicate that those who called Herzl a dreamer, and Herzl's plans chimerical, were not far wrong. That is how Zionism must have appeared to the objective onlooker. But not all Jews could be objective in the matter of national revival. The adoption of Zionism as a goal by so many Jews can be explained not only negatively, by the depth of their hurt over what was happening in Europe—the persecutions in the east and the anti-Semitism in the west—but even more by the creative ferment of the age-old, unforgotten, and unforgettable hope of a return to national life. The fervor and the clamor of the opposition equally show that the opponents of Zionism appreciated the depth of feeling upon which the new movement rested. Such opponents argued vehemently that Jewish nationalism was a thing of the past and that its revival would interfere with the universalist mission of the Jews. This was the view of Isaac M. Wise, the leader of Reform Judaism in the United States, who denounced Zionism with all his customary vigor. Moreover, Wise and others asserted, Zionism laid the Jews open to the charge of disloyalty to the country in which they had their home. It was a fatuous argument, one that did not justify the heat with which it was advanced; the fact was then already obvious that anti-Semites did not need this additional "reason" and that others would not use it.

Most Jews, however, though sympathetic to the aims of Zionism and engaged by the leadership of Theodor Herzl, reacted in typically human fashion to a cause that required the expenditure of effort and energy—they were content to discuss Zionism's evocation of the old hopes without doing much to realize them. There was, indeed, little enough that anyone could do. Local clubs were established in every major city in Europe and America; and federations of such clubs were organized on a nation-wide scale in every country.

Zionism carried on vigorous propaganda: debating, theorizing, educating, and collecting small sums in dues and donations. Its chief function was to keep the hope of restoration alive in the older people, and to stir pride in the Jewish past and dreams of the Jewish future in the young. But there was little that was tangible about Zionism at that time. The only place where the appearance of Zionism on the world Jewish scene made a practical difference was in Palestine itself. There, the few colonies that had been established by the idealistic pioneers of the previous thirty years had begun to show signs of despair over the meager results of their labors and the inadequate support they had been receiving from the Lovers of Zion. Baron Edmond de Rothschild had helped, and in the 1890's, so had the newly-founded ICA. The colonists had proved that Jews could overcome major obstacles and become farmers on highly unpromising soil, provided they had an ideal beyond self to stimulate their interest and keep it alive. Their experience had also proved that a country neglected for centuries could not be revived without great and constant idealistic support. Now Zionism appeared, and quite apart from the few thousand additional colonists who responded to its call and came to join in the revival of the land, it offered the necessary encouragement and promise of support. Among the more hopeful signs Miss Szold recorded for the year 1900 was the fact that Zionism was being taken more seriously and that settlement in Palestine was becoming well established and promising.

4. THE ECONOMIC PROBLEMS OF THE IMMIGRANTS

The migration to Palestine had no perceptible effects on the flow of emigrants from eastern Europe to other parts of the world, especially to the United States. In fact, at the turn of the century, this migration was still on the increase; the problems of the immigrants and the problems they raised for the older strata of the Jewish population continued to agitate mind and spirit and to lay the foundation of changes destined to take place within the next half century. For it must never be forgotten that the immigrants came in most countries into an existing and ongoing Jewish life. They did not start Jewish life anew. Even in such sparsely settled countries as South Africa and Australia, Jewish community life had already been functioning for decades, and the newcomers had to fit themselves into established patterns. A completely free hand, the opportunity to make an entirely new start, was possible only in some Latin American countries where the older Jewish population was small and of the Sephardic tradition and where, in addition, the newcomers settled in groups by themselves, either in farming communities sponsored by ICA, or if in the cities, in groups that had little to do with the Jews already there. Such countries as England and the United States, on the other hand, had Jewish communities with a history and more or less established traditions by which the newcomers were strongly affected. The extent to which the newcomers, in their turn, could modify existing traditions depended on the spirit of the country in general as well as on the strength of the Jewish communal organization and the vigor of its traditional life. The differences to be noted between Britain and the United States, at the end of two generations of joint labor by the older and the newer strata of their respective Jewish populations, must be accounted as the results of the different conditions the newcomers found in the two countries.

The problems raised or intensified by the new immigration fall naturally into three categories: economic, social, and religio-cultural. In actual life none of these problems is easily separable from the others. The nature and severity of his economic struggle made it difficult for the immigrant to tell which aspect of his new life he found most distressing: the rapid tempo of work in his new home as contrasted with the leisurely manner of working to which he had previously been accustomed; the all-pervading, unashamed acquisitiveness, with the rewards of success entailing a complete reversal of social status; or the apparent necessity of giving up his old cultural and religious values and customs in order to attain a degree of comfort and security. From the viewpoint of the community's Jewishness, the difficulties encountered in making a satisfactory adjustment of the immigrants' religious and cultural attitudes were ultimately to prove the most important. But the economic problems were the most immediately pressing and had to be solved first.

When the new immigration started, practically all the countries to which newcomers flowed were in the midst of rapid industrial expansion. Factories in crowded cities offered the greatest opportunity to large numbers of rather unskilled workers who needed immediate means of earning a livelihood. As the nineteenth century drew to its close, the possibilities for peddling, and eventually opening local stores, decreased. A sociologist points to a notable difference between the opportunities open to the east European immigrants and those that had been open to the immigrants who preceded them: the latter had been able to rise to a higher economic and social status within half a generation; the east European immigrants took a full generation to achieve the same goal.

The factories drew them in. Some had had a certain amount of experience in the slowly developing industries of eastern Europe; most had had none. Many of the immigrants were young people who had had nothing at all to look forward to in Russia and Rumania. Others, a considerable number, would have joined the large—altogether too large—class of petty traders in the small Russian towns; it was practically all that the east European economy had permitted them to do. And still others, comparatively many, were far advanced in their studies at the *yeshivot* and might have become religious functionaries of one sort or another; east European Jewry needed many such functionaries, but the United States needed only a few. In the United States the immigrants, all alike, became factory workers, producing a large variety of articles, chiefly garments.

A modern historian of labor has listed the reasons why so many immigrants of those years went into the needle trades. Many had been tailors in the old country, and those who had not plied the needle there could quickly learn to do so here; new machinery made it a skill easily acquired. The hours of work were long—a twelve-hour day was not at all unusual in the factories at the end of the nineteenth century—but the work itself did not call for the type of muscular exertion of which these men and women were incapable. Most of the factory owners were Jews, and even if of a different tradition and upbringing, a person hailing from eastern Europe and therefore uneasy in the company of non-Jews could feel somewhat at home with them. It was even possible to find shops in the needle industry which kept closed on the Sabbath. Finally, with the industry as then organized, it was possible to graduate, within a fairly short time, into a semblance of independence despite one's very limited capital.

It has been estimated that between 1880 and 1914 two thirds of the Jewish immigrants from eastern Europe began their American experience by entering the needle trades; but whatever industry they joined, not many of these immigrants expected to remain merely workers in a shop. Some labored feverishly to amass the modest sum necessary in those days to set themselves up as subcontractors in crowded back rooms, with a few, more recent immigrants as workers. This practice aggravated the already unspeakable sweatshop conditions in the big industrial cities; yet it had its brighter side too, for it was the first step up the ladder of success. Others dreamed of escaping the atmosphere of the clothing or cigar factory by going into "business," if only as pushcart peddlers on the overcrowded streets or as storekeepers in hole-in-the-wall shops from which they could dispense soft drinks or needles and thread. Still others, more intellectually inclined, or lacking the inner drive and sometimes the toughness essential for success in the existing competitive situation, succeeded after incredible efforts, after much hardship and self-sacrifice, in obtaining an education and entering a profession. Such hopes were certainly not realized in every case. Most of the immigrants eventually became resigned to the inescapable lot of wearing labor. Their hopes of success were transferred to their children, and their personal disappointments were expressed in dreams of social change.

The physical relocation of so large a segment of the world's Jewish population represented a normalization, even as it created an anomaly. The normalization was in the area of economic life, the Jews now becoming artisans in large and growing numbers. At the same time, these new artisans, still imbued with social and intellectual values that most other workers did not possess, were somewhat out of place in the ranks of labor. This fact was of importance not only for the emergent labor movement but also for the social and religious development of the Jewish community.

Before the 1900's, it seemed difficult to organize the Jewish workers into labor unions. Little could be done with them until they learned that their chances for improvement lay not outside the shop, but within it. Moreover, the Jewish worker's religious training and his experiences as a Jew in the old country had taught him to view his situation in terms of broad universal issues. Unionism merely for the improvement of his personal lot failed to fire his imagination. He had to be aroused by calls to his sense of justice and appeals on the basis of human dignity. He still remembered what he had learned in the *heder* of the prophetic message against the oppression of the poor. Craft unionism, as advocated by the American Federation of Labor under the leadership of Samuel Gompers, a fellow Jewish immigrant, seemed to the average Jewish worker to lack intellectual and spiritual foundations. It stood for a gradual improvement in the physical situation of the worker, while leaving basic conditions unchallenged. Many Jews sought a better mixture of the practical and the idealistic.

Jewish labor could be moved by ideas. Every so often an intellectual would be called in to encourage an embattled group—thus Abraham Cahan had been called in during a tailors' strike in 1884—but there was no continuous contact between such leaders and the workers. At length, a small number of Jewish intellectuals decided to take matters in hand. Several of them had some knowledge of, or experience in, labor and socialist movements in Europe; others, workers like the people they wished to organize, at the same time were pursuing professional courses in American colleges. In 1888 they founded the United Hebrew Trades, and within two years, enrolled twenty-two unions with a membership of about six thousand workers, all of whom were employed in New York City. Jewish labor, as has been repeatedly pointed out, was thus organized from the top down.

It was one thing to organize the Jewish workers into unions; it was quite another to give them ideological guidance. The last fifteen years of the nineteenth century resounded with quarrels within the ranks of Jewish labor. The question that came repeatedly to the fore, then and in later years as well, was whether labor should be a tool of socialist theory or socialism the goal of a political party furthering the interests of labor. The plays and counterplays of radical theoreticians worked havoc with unionism among the Jews. What Daniel DeLeon and his Socialist Labor Party did to the Jewish unions of the last decade of the century was to be repeated under more ominous circumstances some thirty years later when the issue of communism threatened to wreck the labor unions, especially those in the needle trades. On both occasions, moderate leadership and principled journalism turned the tide.

5. THE CULTURE OF THE TRANSPLANTED

Economic and political interests were of course important in the life of the east European Jewish immigrant; but they alone cannot explain his attitudes, nor can they explain those of the next generation. The immigrant brought with him ideas that had been spreading in his old environment, modified them, and developed them further in accordance with the demands of the new. This is why the history of the Jews in the United States, and in other countries as well, during the past two generations, cannot be fully understood without recognizing the transformation that Jewish life had begun to undergo in eastern Europe at the very time the great migration began.

By the middle of the nineteenth century, the literary-cultural movement that went by the name of *Haskalah* (Enlightenment) had become strongly entrenched in the larger Jewish communities of the Russian Pale of Settlement. In fact, in an eagerness for western culture amounting almost to a denial of Jewish loyalties, the upper middle class was already going beyond *Haskalah*. The lower middle class and the workers, especially those who lived in the smaller towns and villages, continued to be guided by ancient tradition; Jewish values certainly did not lose their force among them. Nonetheless, as a peripheral result of *Haskalah,* the organized Jewish communities, the old customs and habits, were suffering a perceptible loss of authority.

There were several ways in which this new spirit manifested itself, at the very time that emigration was reaching its height. The new literature, which had been produced during the generation or two before, was not so much secular as nonreligious and nonlegalistic. It was written not for the talmudical scholar but for the man of average intelligence and Jewish education—a fact that in itself represented a radical change in the east European literary tradition. The new Jewish literature in Germany, generally speaking, represented historical research with apologetic overtones; the east European Jewish community, on the other hand, more populous, closer to the literary sources of Judaism, living in the midst of a less attractive cultural environment, had begun to produce a vital literature of a different kind.

The most striking external characteristic of this new Jewish literature was the fact that it functioned in two languages: Yiddish and Hebrew. The appearance of a Yiddish literature was one of the extraordinary developments of Jewish life in the nineteenth century. By the century's end, Yiddish literature had already gone through two stages and was well along on the third. Early in the century its activity had been rather timid: Yiddish works, whether pro-Hasidic or anti-Hasidic, pietistic or urging *Haskalah,* were frequently not even printed, but circulated in manuscript. Authors and readers were almost shamefaced about seeming to displace Hebrew as the literary language of the Jewish people. This stage was followed, about the middle of the century, by a period when Yiddish literature reached out for an audience. Abandoning all pretense to literary respectability, which at that time and place demanded intellectualism, pietism, or both, Yiddish authors began writing for the common people either frankly to entertain them or subtly to criticize their intellectually or economically better-placed fellows. These two periods of its growth saw Yiddish literature develop in social perception, expand in vocabulary, and gain refinement in style. In the final quarter of the century Yiddish literature emerged into full bloom, with respected authors, numerous readers, and such deep-seated self-esteem that its protagonists raised the question whether Yiddish rather than Hebrew was not the proper language for Jews to call their own.

The three men whose magic pens raised Yiddish literature to a recognized position were Shalom Jacob Abramovitch (1836-1917), better known under his pen name Mendele Mokher Sefarim, Shalom Rabinowitz (1859-1916), famous under the pen name Shalom Aleichem, and Isaac Loeb Peretz (1851-1915). The first led the way in making a keen, poetic, plastic instrument out of the folk language, burdened as it had been with heavy Hebrew idioms and vague turns of phrase. Because of this, as well as because he was the oldest of the group of Yiddish writers, he came to be known as the grandfather of Yiddish literature. Both he and Shalom Aleichem used satire and humor—Mendele more of the former and Shalom Aleichem more of the latter—to portray the life and struggles of the east European Jew who lived cooped up in the Pale of Settlement. Peretz was closer to the Hasidic tradition and proved to be an inspiring teller of moving and profound tales. All three of these men, writing of the masses, if not quite for the masses, displayed a love of Judaism and Jewish life that placed them far above their contemporaries and their immediate successors.

Each of the three wrote in Hebrew as well. Generally speaking, the division in the users of the languages down to the emergence of Zionism, and even for the decade beyond, was in terms of the instrument of expression rather than in terms of sources of inspiration, of social background, or of goals for Jewish life. In fact, because Hebrew literature in the first three quarters of the nineteenth century was addressed to the more intellectual class, it was much more critical than was the Yiddish literature of the time. Holding aloft the banner of enlightenment, the deeply social Hebrew writers of the mid-nineteenth century had openly and bitingly criticized various aspects of Jewish life: the exclusive concern with religion, which had till then been the sole mark of culture among the Jews; the communal leadership, which had become arrogant; the prevailing religiosity, which had become barren; and the narrowness of the bounds within which the current educational system had been keeping the minds of the young at the very time when the world's broad culture was being made available to them. One need but think of Judah Loeb Gordon (1829-1892) who in his historical poems romanticized and glorified the Jewish past and in his lyrical poems heaped scorn upon the present. His contemporary, the novelist Peretz Smolenskin (1842-1885) seemed equally obsessed by the hypocrisy and stupidity he thought he found in Jewish life.

As with so much else in east European Jewish life, the fateful years 1881 and 1882 brought a change also in the temper and content of Hebrew literature. The czarist whip awakened the cosmopolitan, Russophile, *Haskalah*-minded Jews from their dreams of entering European civilization through the door of freedom which they were sure would soon open in Russia. That door was now firmly shut in their faces. Deeply hurt, disillusioned, they turned back to Jewish life and searched within themselves for ways of rebuilding it. But such ways were not easy to find. They could not abandon the hope of becoming part of cultured Europe; nor could they rebuild the bridge to the religious milieu they had left behind. Looking back, some of the very men who had been most critical of old-fashioned Jewish life—Gordon, for example—now admitted that it had had beauty and spirituality. But looking ahead, they saw a dark and pathless jungle.

The Hebrew literature produced by these men and by their contemporaries gives the impression of an aimless search by the spiritually uprooted. Its marvelously tuneful poetry, magnificent in its imagery, superb in its use of the Hebrew language so recently restored to active life, was either nostalgic or heroic; it wept or fulminated; but it offered no tangible goal, no acceptable program. Chaim Nachman Bialik (1873-1934) to this day thrills the reader of his poetry with his evocations of the spiritual roots of Jewish life and his stirring descriptions of how past generations tried to free themselves from the curses of tradition and exile that enchained them. Saul Tchernichovsky (1875-1943) urged strength and physical beauty—the Greek ideal —in place of the presumably debilitating devotion to study and tradition that had characterized Jewish life. No one— novelist, poet, or writer of mighty Hebrew prose—set forth a policy or offered a plan. Merely to protest against fate and to deny the verdicts of history is not a program for the future. It is generally conceded that Mordecai Zeev Feierberg's story *"Le'an"* ("Whither") symbolizes the plight of the Jewish intellectual of the period—defiantly broken with the past, and left with no place to go.

The Hovevei Tsiyon did, to be sure, suggest a program, namely, the solution of personal and Jewish problems by settlement, as farmers, in the Holy Land. But it seemed so far-fetched, so impractical, that it was shrugged off as a dream. BILU and the colonists were admired and discussed in the new Hebrew periodicals, but no one considered the movement as a source of hope for the solution of the physical or spiritual problems the Jews faced.

One voice, raised at the beginning of the last decade of the nineteenth century, claimed special attention. In a Hebrew more simple and beautiful than any prose the generation had yet produced, in terms that challenged and electrified his readers, Asher Ginzberg (1856-1927), under the pen name Ahad Ha'Am, began a series of essays to interpret the modern Jew to himself. Neither ghetto nor assimilation was the proper program for a self-respecting people. The aim and object of Jewish life was the preservation of the Jewish spirit. This could be achieved in a culturally independent Jewish community in Palestine; it could never be achieved in a physical or spiritual ghetto, or by Jews eager to lose themselves among the nations. Ahad Ha'Am was deeply interested in the Palestinian effort because of the spiritual results that he hoped it would yield. But this effort could not be enough. More important for the time being was the revival among the Jews of the diaspora of those cultural values that were the essence of Jewishness. These were imbedded in the Hebrew language and its literature. Ahad Ha'Am's program thus called for a cultural renaissance in the diaspora, and a physical renaissance in Palestine. When Theodor Herzl's call came, toward the end of the same decade, Ahad Ha'Am could greet it only halfheartedly; it corresponded to only half his pro-

gram, to the half, moreover, that he considered less important. But it was from the ideas of both these men—of
Theodor Herzl as well as Ahad Ha'Am—and, from their
programs for revitalizing Jewish life, that Hebrew writers
soon took fire, drew new meaning, renewed faith.

To what extent did all this literary and intellectual activity, this criticism of and break with the past, affect the
Jewish population of eastern Europe? It took time for the
new currents of thought to penetrate the vast majority of
the east European Jewish population. The majority of those
actual readers who had been brought up close to, or within,
the institutions criticized knew that the accusations were
exaggerated intentionally, to stimulate reform rather than
to destroy. Other readers, pious traditionalists, looked upon
all this literature, whether Yiddish or Hebrew, as impious
nonsense. Readers of both types were likely to be elderly,
somewhat set in their ways, and unwilling to uproot themselves except under most unusual conditions. Consequently,
the earlier the date of emigration from eastern Europe, the
fewer the people of conservative nature to be found among
the migrants.

In other segments of the Jewish population rebelliousness
against religious restraint was more actively fed by critical
literary and cultural currents. Many Jews had, in any case,
already lost patience with the traditional Jewish modes of
thought and life. Many Jewish intellectuals hungered for
western culture; but with rare exceptions, the gates of Russian universities were closed to them. Many went to western
universities, many others were self-taught. But wherever
they were educated, the rationalism of the day prevailed.
These intellectuals provided the leadership for the variety
of ideological groups into which the sons and daughters
of the Jewish middle and working classes flocked. They
joined the secret revolutionary societies that aimed to west-
ernize and democratize the Russian state. They organized
the Bund (1897), which represented, among the Jewish
workers, the revolutionary strivings of Russian socialism

while recognizing the folk—though not the national—character of the Jewish population and appealing to it through the Yiddish language. Others among the intellectuals, imbued with deeper Jewish loyalties, were captivated by the theory of the Jewish historian Simon Dubnow (1860-1942), who contended that diaspora Jewry needed no political center to lead a national life, but could continue to live, as it had lived for almost two thousand years, united by its culture in a unique spiritual nationalism. Finally, Russian Jewish intellectuals were also among the first to respond with enthusiasm to Herzl's call on behalf of political nationalism. All these groups, it must be emphasized, represented departures, in greater or lesser degrees, from the purely religious character of Jewish life and all that it meant in terms of customs, learning, and spiritual values.

Russian Jewish youth did not consist entirely of rebellious intellectuals. The working people and the small-town and village Jews continued to send their sons to *heder,* where they became acquainted with the elements of Judaism. Eventually, however, they too heard the clamor of the battle for the Jewish mind which was being waged in eastern Europe. A neighbor's intellectual son or daughter, temporarily returned from studying in the big city, the local subscriber to a newspaper, visitors, even peddlers, could plant the seeds of doubt, or offer a glimpse into a new, different, and therefore more alluring world. The old ways, being deeply rooted, prevailed as long as the younger people remained in the old environment; thus few changes were perceptible for another decade or two. But the younger people were the very element of the Jewish population to whom emigration made the strongest appeal. They emigrated, and having emigrated, were subjected not only to the upsetting effects of a completely changed environment and the intoxicating sense of freedom from parental and religious control, but also to the influence of newspapers, books, ideas, and currents of thought that fitted in with their new-found freedom and their natural desire for rapid adjustment. The young Jewish emigrant, equipped only with his *heder* education, heard of the conflict, then at its height, between science and religion. Spinoza and Spencer, Darwin and Marx, replaced the biblical heroes and the midrashic stories absorbed in his old home. He learned that the validity of the manner of life that his home town's rabbi represented had long been disputed. The religion upon which he had been brought up appeared to have no relevance to the economic and social problems that beset him. On the other hand, what he saw and what he was told of Reform Judaism, the new, western religious attitude, appeared strange, alien, and even more irrelevant. Emigrants from eastern Europe were, therefore, divided into two types. The older among them, more fixed in habits of mind and spirit, hungry for accustomed forms and ways, made every effort to transplant to the new land the synagogue and other communal institutions that existed in the old. But the younger people followed their intellectual leaders along the new paths that were supposed to lead to happier promised lands.

6. THE PROBLEM OF RELIGION
IN AN AGE OF RATIONALISM

The cleavage between old and new religious attitudes was more evident in the United States than in other countries. To some extent this was due to the unusual sharpness of the economic struggle in which the newer immigration was involved. It was due also and above all to the fact that traditionalism in general was weaker in America than in other predominantly Anglo-Saxon countries. In Britain, the immigrants also went through a period of social and religious conflict; but the spiritual dislocation was not as sharp, primarily because of the better communal and religious organization the immigrants found already in existence, and the greater regard for tradition which characterized the old population and with which the newcomers quickly fell in line.

In the United States, by the end of the nineteenth century, the immigrants of the so-called second migration, that of the period before 1880, had become adjusted to life in America. Economically, linguistically, and politically, they considered themselves fully acclimatized citizens, and they were so considered by their Christian neighbors. In large part, the Jews of 1880 were second and even third generation Americans, so that many were far removed from the intellectual outlook and emotional attachments of east European Jewry. But they had not fully succeeded in solving their religious and cultural problems.

By the end of the century, the religious life of the older strata of the Jewish population already showed the three groupings that have maintained their identity to this day. Many vain attempts to establish a nation-wide union of congregations had been made by the devoted and far-sighted Isaac Leeser (1806-1868) and by the energetic Isaac M. Wise (1819-1900). The latter did succeed in establishing a union of congregations (1873) in the Middle West as well as a college for the training of rabbis, the Hebrew Union College, in Cincinnati (1875). For a decade, it still seemed possible that these organizations could serve as a nucleus for union. In 1885, however, Wise and his colleagues, some of them more radical than he, joined in the formulation of the Pittsburgh Platform, which voiced principles more extreme than any Reformist trends then existing in Europe. In immediate reaction, Sabato Morais (1823-1897), Leeser's successor as minister of Philadelphia's Mikveh Israel Congregation, and a number of other rabbis and lay leaders of more traditional views, began working for similar institutions to counteract Reform. The Jewish Theological Seminary of America was founded in 1886. It was hoped that all the tradition-loving elements of the Jewish community in the United States would group themselves around it. But it became clear within a very few years that a considerable part of the Jewish population was not content with the program of the Seminary and hardly satisfied with the moderate views of those who sponsored it. The growing immigration from eastern Europe after 1880 had resulted in the establishment of numerous synagogues and the arrival of many rabbis who wanted neither affiliation nor even co-operation with the existing institutions. At the turn of the century, while Reform and traditionalist pulpits resounded with sectarian disputation, the more recent immigrants disdainfully turned away from both.

A large number of these immigrants remained untouched by any religious viewpoint. The Americanized Jewish population was no more immune than the immigrant group to the allurements of current nonreligious and antireligious ideas. The former did not, on the whole, find Karl Marx as attractive as the younger immigrants found him; but the other ingredients of nineteenth-century intellectualism affected them quite as much as the immigrants. Rationalism, humanism, and even atheism found many devotees. The Ethical Culture movement (1876), founded by Felix Adler (1851-1933), a former student for the Reform rabbinate, attracted many Jews. Religion had ceased to be the center of Jewish life in the sense in which it had been its focus for millennia.

The growing religious indifference was blamed then, as it has been ever since, on the inadequacy of existing means for transmitting Jewish knowledge. From the very beginning, the Jewish population made valiant efforts to overcome the difficulties in the way of giving their children a Jewish education. Toward the middle of the nineteenth century, it had looked as though the solution might be the all-day Jewish school with a curriculum of both secular and religious subjects. The development of the public school system, however, put an end to this experiment. Some traditionalist synagogues, in various parts of the country, established afternoon religious schools; others, schools that met for a few hours on Saturday and Sunday. The basic institution to emerge during the mid-nineteenth century was the

Sabbath school, or Sunday school. Through the Union of American Hebrew Congregations, the Reform group tried to co-ordinate the educational efforts of these schools, and founded the Sabbath School Union in 1886. As Reform Judaism was to learn in the decades to come, it was naïve to imagine that a few hours a week would suffice to transmit any appreciable part of the vast Jewish cultural heritage.

The east European immigrants, accustomed to a much more profound and extensive Jewish education, were compelled to seek a solution of their own. By the end of the nineteenth century, they were employing three methods of achieving their goal. One was an Old World institution, the *heder*. It became, when transported to the United States, an afternoon school conducted usually in a dingy room by a person frequently ill-equipped for his task and almost always unable to cope with his charges. A second method was that of the "private rebbe," an itinerant peddler of instruction, who went from home to home and gave the boy of the house a few minutes of daily Hebrew reading practice. Rarely going beyond mechanical reading, presumably preparatory to the boy's participation in the synagogue service, this could hardly be called Jewish education.

The third and most promising means of transmitting Jewish education in the last part of the century was the *Talmud Torah*. Like the *heder,* it was an institution transported from eastern Europe. After undergoing some changes, it became a semipublic afternoon school, organized and supervised by responsible Jews of a neighborhood, using a course of study with gradations and goals appropriate for its time and people, and employing as good a staff of teachers as was then available. The Machzikei Talmud Torah in New York and a similar school in Chicago were established in 1883 and served as models for other cities. In 1886, the Etz Chaim school was established in New York with a more ambitious course of study, including Talmud; thus the foundations were laid for a rabbinical *yeshivah.*

With elementary education making comparatively little progress, it was clear that adult education must be called upon to help redeem the situation. In the spring of 1888, representative leaders of Jewish religion and culture met in Philadelphia to establish the Jewish Publication Society for the production of Jewish reading material in the English language. This idea, too, had been thought of long before by the spiritually alert Isaac Leeser. But his effort (1845-1851) as well as another, in the 1870's, had failed. Better organization, wider sponsorship, the availability of more popular books and authors, and a larger public from which to draw members contributed to the greater success of the third effort. Under the active guidance of Mayer Sulzberger, and with Henrietta Szold as its editor-secretary, the Jewish Publication Society introduced Israel Zangwill to the English-reading world, and also before the end of the century, published a translation of Heinrich Graetz's *History of the Jews* in a somewhat abbreviated form. Meant to serve the needs of the second and third generations of the already-established population, the Jewish Publication Society became an increasingly potent force in the supplementary Jewish education of almost all strata of the American Jewish community.

Despite these valiant efforts begun in the latter part of the nineteenth century and continued into the twentieth, it must be admitted that the new American Jewish generation was growing up without firm attachments to Judaism and its traditions. The reasons for this—it is worth re-emphasizing—were the antireligious climate of the period, the social and economic problems that beset the immigrant parents, the cultural cleavage between the generations, the hopes the New World engendered and the opportunities it offered, and the social messianism that replaced the old religious one. The Jewish home, under the guidance of immigrant parents, no longer served as the training ground for education in the old values.

7. AMERICANIZATION AND PHILANTHROPY

Another long-existing institution also underwent a conscious transformation. Social and literary clubs for Jewish young people had been in existence since the 1840's. In the 1850's, such clubs reorganized themselves into Young Men's Hebrew Associations. The literary aspects of the clubs had been rather superficial before; their Hebrew aspect meant just as little now. But the YMHA's, and the YWHA's, were useful in that they served as meeting places for Jewish youth. Debates, dances, musicals, theatricals, and amateur athletics were conducted in them. They offered lectures and courses on Jewish subjects established libraries, and took note of holidays and special Jewish events. Frequently, they housed Sabbath and weekday schools for the poorer Jewish children. The coming of the new immigrants, moreover, provided the score or more of such institutions throughout the country with opportunities to join in the Americanization program that the older stratum of the Jewish population began to consider all-important.

All segments of the Jewish population were interested in the work of Americanization. The newly-arrived, being for the most part young, ambitious, and intellectually hungry, knew that the sooner they acquired the language and manners of America the sooner they would feel, and they hoped, be made to feel, at home. They enrolled in classes in English and quickly Americanized their names and clothes and aped what they could see of the manners of America. It takes almost no imagination to realize that progress in these respects did not at once ease the sense of strangeness and uprootedness that the immigrants felt. The adult immigrant needed time to forget the environment and give up the habits of mind and body in which he had been reared, and inwardly to accept the new way of life.

Moreover, one does not learn to feel at home; he must be made to feel at home. The American Jewish population of

longer standing, for its part, did all it could for the immigrant, all except take him to its bosom. Humanly speaking,
one could hardly have expected the older Americans to treat
as equals people of strange language and customs, poverty-
stricken, and in many cases, somewhat foreign in manners.
Amid the growing trend to define aristocracy in terms of
wealth and length of American residence—operative within
Jewish groups as well as in Christian society—the Jewish
immigrant appeared to be lowering the standing of older
Jewish residents. Not that Jews of any type or kind would
under any circumstances have been accepted in the Gentile
society of that day, but the presence of the immigrants served
as an excuse for the widespread practice of exclusion. The
Jewish Americans of long residence more than suspected that
their non-Jewish neighbors lumped all Jews together. Some
impatience and bitterness were therefore inevitable.

Classes in English and in citizenship, public lectures in
Yiddish and in English, reading rooms and recreation facilities for young and old—these and dozens of other means
were used in the drive to Americanize the immigrants in as
short a time as possible. In New York, the Educational Alliance was a magnificent institution built, for this purpose,
in the heart of the East Side immigrant district. Similar
buildings were erected in other large cities. Incomparable
social service work was done by such institutions as the
Henry Street Settlement in New York, directed by Lillian
D. Wald, and Hull House in Chicago, directed by Jane
Addams. These settlement houses and others like them
admirably performed many services in the midst of the
city slums and pioneered in social work that proved of
great advantage to the entire community. The National
Council of Jewish Women, organized in 1893, also plunged
into the work in behalf of the immigrants. Its members were
active in the settlements; its chapters took under their care
children who showed signs of becoming delinquent and
charged themselves with the protection of girl immigrants.

There was, of course, no limit to activities of a charitable nature. Long before the beginnings of the east European immigrations, the Jews of the United States had established a network of charitable institutions. Indeed, as religion became progressively less important as a bond of union among all Jews, charity emerged, to some extent, as a substitute for it. The vast, constantly growing, immigrant population multiplied old problems and created many new ones. Hospital and orphanage facilities had to be expanded; direct support had to be provided to prevent homes from breaking up; stranded people had to be helped. The challenge to the established Jewish community was such as to confront it with the alternative of allowing its charity system to break under the strain or developing philanthropy to such an extent as to lead the entire field. The Jews of the United States met all philanthropic emergencies.

Charity functioned exceedingly well. Co-operation, planning, the scientific approach, the substitution of professional for volunteer help, the supervision of workers—these and other evidences of efficiency were introduced in its various areas of activity. Even the need to avoid wastefulness in the collection of funds was not lost sight of. Beginning with Boston in 1895 and Cincinnati in 1896, federations of Jewish charity organizations developed in most of the larger cities. By 1900 a national conference of Jewish charities met annually. One important reason for this progress was the presence in the Jewish community of excellent leadership in the field: Morris Loeb (1863-1912) and Lee K. Frankel (1867-1931), for example, among the social experts, and Jacob H. Schiff (1847-1920), Adolph Lewisohn (1849-1938), and Daniel Guggenheim (1856-1930) among the philanthropists. The fact to remember, however, is that the entire Jewish community was behind these leaders. There was a challenge, and it was met in the traditional Jewish fashion, though by methods as different and as complex as were the problems that faced the Jews of that day.

The situation was, of course, not a happy one for the beneficiaries of charitable activity. They were not so much ungrateful as resentful. All too frequently it was the givers who were really at fault. Condescension, by the kind ladies who did volunteer work in the settlements, by the men who would rather work *for* the immigrants than with them, was often obvious. No charitable institutions of those days invited representation on their boards from among the people who were most concerned. The immigrants and everything that characterized them, sometimes including their religion, were disparaged. They were asked to break completely with their past, a request that could not work with the older people but succeeded with their children, thus multiplying rather than decreasing the problems of the home. To natural economic and cultural cleavages there was thus added a social cleavage that went even deeper. The breach between the "uptowners" and the "downtowners," as they were known in New York—and similar groups with similar names elsewhere in the country—was not to be healed until, during the lifetime of the second American generation of the twentieth century, the total situation was transformed.

Mutual irritation drove the immigrants back upon their own resources. It encouraged the immigrants' natural tendency to re-establish in their new homes the various institutions to which they had been accustomed. But completely transferring the east European small town proved impossible. All the immigrants were left with to bridge the miles and the centuries, the manners and the hopes, were the synagogue and that artificial re-creation of old world society which came to be known as the *landsmanshaft* lodge. At the meetings of the latter, as in the traditions of the former, the immigrant could relive temporarily the good old days when life was simpler and less upsetting. Besides, such organizations served as resources for mutual help. Rather than turn in time of need to the established "charities," with their searching and degrading investigations, the immigrants preferred to turn to assistance funds of their own. Before long they began establishing new institutions. The Russian

Jews of New York, for example, as early as 1892, founded the Hebrew Free Loan Society with a capital of ninety-five dollars; the Society is still in existence, though many of its imitators in other large cities no longer are, and proudly boasts of having lost in bad loans throughout its career no more than one half of one per cent of its total funds, which by the 1950's ran into half a million dollars. So, too, before the century came to an end, hospitals, old age homes, and orphanages were founded by east European Jews in various parts of the country. The avowed reasons for such duplication of existing institutions were that the old ones did not make the east European Jew feel at home, that they provided no Jewish atmosphere, that they did not observe the dietary laws. Henrietta Szold, in her *Year Book* review of the close of the century, refers to the charge that this duplication was unnecessary by saying that it may have been ill-advised but that it was certainly not discreditable.

The course of events in other parts of the world was in many respects no different from that in the United States. Everywhere except in eastern Europe, the old, established Jewish populations, despite some evidences of latent anti-Semitism among their neighbors, enjoyed a rather increased sense of at-homeness, while the newcomers among them struggled hard to overcome their economic and spiritual dislocations. Israel Zangwill's charming sketches of Jewish life in London's crowded Whitechapel could as easily have reflected New York's East Side. The continental cities of western Europe did not have such problems to the same extent. The German police knew how, quite unofficially, to discourage immigrants from settling in that country. France and the other west European states offered comparatively few economic opportunities. Of non-European countries, South Africa began to attract a considerable number of immigrants—for some reason, mostly Lithuanian Jews—because it offered the greatest promise of opportunity and freedom. Similar reasons made Canada another goal of immigration. Thus, the foundations were laid, and the English-speaking countries were eventually to become the centers of Jewish population.

Available estimates indicate the Jewish population of the world in the year 1900 was slightly over 11,500,000, and stood at the following approximate figures:

United States	1,058,000
Canada	16,000
Latin America	9,700
Russia	5,700,000
Austria-Hungary	1,870,000
Rumania	1,300,000
Germany	568,000
Turkey	350,000
United Kingdom	148,000
Netherlands	97,000
France	72,000
Italy	50,000
Bulgaria	22,600
Rest of Europe	33,650
Northern Africa	320,000
South Africa	10,000
Asia (except Turkey)	60,000

This was the body, scattered and weak, of the Jewish people which was destined to meet the numerous revolutionary changes of the next half-century. If the threats of disintegration and tragedy were already visible, the forces to counterbalance them were also asserting themselves. Looking back upon the final years of the old century, one cannot help noting that old hopes were being revived, new organizations were being created, efforts at adjustment were never slackened, ingrained values were gaining strength. These were some of the characteristics with which the Jews entered a new and more dangerous age.

II

. . . .

Experiments in Adjustment

. . . .

1. FOR A MEASURE OF SECURITY

The new century was merely a date on the calendar; it did not mark any sudden transformation in the ways of the world or any alleviation of the problems that faced mankind. As far as the Jews were concerned, the changes that were taking place were at the time imperceptible. Equally imperceptible and just as unabating were the efforts, physical and spiritual, that ongoing events aroused among Jews of all types and classes.

Emigration from eastern Europe continued; indeed, it increased. The average annual immigration of Jews to the United States between 1900 and 1913 exceeded 100,000. Jewish migration to other parts of the world was relatively as large. Everywhere, this sharpened the problems of Jewish relations with the non-Jewish population and of relations within the Jewish community. In the United States, on a number of occasions, Congress passed restrictive immigration measures in the form of literacy tests (1896, 1913, 1915, 1917), which were vetoed by the presidents. In Great Britain, the labor unions were persuaded that immigrants competed unfairly with native labor and lowered the standard of living. A parliamentary commission held hearings and a restrictive law was passed; but the government did little to enforce it. Immediate danger of a closing of the gates was thus averted, but the Jews of older residence were impressed with the need to do something to avert its recurrence.

If the irritations incident to the arrival of large numbers of immigrants could not be averted, they could, it was believed in some quarters, be mitigated by directing immigrants away from the overcrowded cities. The ICA, of course, continued to function in both North and South America. The Jewish Agricultural Society, in the first ten years of its activity, co-operated with the ICA to settle over three thousand Jewish families on farms in New England, New York, New Jersey, and states farther west. It not only continued to guide these families and give them instruction, but it tried also to give agricultural training to such others as showed some interest in going into farming. But the way of the novice farmers was hard. Frequently, they were compelled to supplement their incomes by taking in summer boarders or by working part time in factories. Frequently, when they came to terms with their new life, it did not appear likely that they would be able to make farmers out of their sons and daughters. With the trend in the general population away from the farm, it seemed rather unreasonable to look for its reversal among Jews.

Even temporary success in this respect was, however, a gain, since it removed that many families from the slums of the cities. Other experiments toward the same end were therefore tried. In 1901 the Industrial Removal Office was established. Its aim was to persuade immigrants to move farther inland in the United States, where opportunities for adjustment might be better. The IRO succeeded, in the course of a very few years, in transferring some 40,000 Jewish immigrants to the smaller towns in the interior. As quickly as these left the eastern seaboard, others took their place. It seemed necessary also to prevent the very debarkation of immigrants in the crowded centers. The wise, kindly, philanthropic Jacob H. Schiff espoused an idea that came to be known as the Galveston Plan because that southern port played the chief role in it. Immigrants were to be persuaded at ports of embarkation in Europe to avoid the eastern seaboard of the United States and to enter the country through the South. It was hoped thereby to shunt considerable numbers into the more sparsely settled portions of the country. The plan began to operate in 1907, and there were indications that it might achieve the objectives sought, when World War I interrupted its development.

Having hurdled the difficulty of transferring themselves from their stepmotherlands to their new homes, the immigrants had to turn to the pressing economic problems of daily living. Earning a livelihood did not come easy. But conflict and uproar was accompanied by quiet adjustment and comparatively rapid acclimatization. Again the progress of events in the United States must serve as the example because it illustrates the process on the largest canvas.

The center of the struggle was the Jewish labor union. As the century opened, the focus of union labor activity was away from ideological disputes and toward the use of unionization for material improvement. Both the United Garment Workers (UGW, organized in 1891) and the International Ladies Garment Workers Union (ILGWU, organized in 1900) finally came into their own during the first decade of the new century, as did the unions of the furriers, capmakers, and others. In one city after another, strikes were productive of greatly improved conditions, and victories heartened the workers and prepared them for the greater struggles to come. Moreover, union efforts now had the sympathy of the liberal elements of the population. It had finally dawned upon people that the factory workers could really not be blamed, as they had been for decades, for the slum conditions in which they lived, as long as the length of the working day sapped their energies and low pay made decent living conditions a luxury.

With the economic revival that followed the comparatively slight depression of 1907, the various needle industries began to prepare for showdown strikes. The most spectacular was the strike of 20,000 girls who worked in shirtwaist factories in New York. It began in November 1909, and had the full sympathy of the New York public. The strike lasted for three months, but it ended in an almost complete victory for the girls. A few months later, in July 1910, workers in the cloak and suit industry went out on strike. In this case, too, employers were forced to yield a substantial victory to the strikers. Especially interesting in this case was the use of public opinion to work a change in the relations between workers and employers. The vast majority of the workers and employers being Jews, both sides were appealed to on the basis of safeguarding the reputation of the Jewish population. Jacob H. Schiff and Louis Marshall, who commanded the respect of all concerned, urged a cessation of the violence that characterized strikes in those days, and arrival at a settlement without waiting for the total surrender of one side or the other. Louis D. Brandeis, then a noted Boston lawyer, worked out a plan for a permanent board of grievance through which all future disputes were to be referred to impartial arbitrators. In modified form, this plan was to remain part of union-employer relations in the needle industries from then on. In time, it spread to other unionized industries as well.

Despite some setbacks, internal wrangling, and constant recriminations between employers and employees, the Jewish labor unions came through the period of World War I strengthened and more popular. The sweatshop was a thing of the past, destroyed less by government action than by labor victories; working conditions were incomparably superior to those of the previous decades; wage rates bore a closer relation than formerly to the cost of living. No one could say any longer that Jews were incapable of unionization. It was, in fact, clear that the Jewish unions were among the strongest and most intelligently led in the United States.

Yet it was already clear by the time of World War I that the needle industries and other trades in which Jews had preponderated to the extent of almost ninety per cent of the workers would not long retain their high Jewish ratio. The large immigration of the century's first decade and a half tended to cover up the fact that the second generation of American Jews was turning to other areas of economic activity. On the whole, it was a period of expansion for small business. Seen in retrospect, it does not appear to have taken long for factory workers and peddlers to turn into grocers, butchers, tinsmiths, cigar-store owners, opticians, and dozens of other kinds of vendors. Some seized the opportunity, because they had the imagination, to enter and develop new fields. Thus, the nascent motion picture industry, still manifesting itself during the century's first decade in little more than penny arcades, was taken hold of by a number of immigrants and turned into a new, vastly popular form of entertainment. Whether economic insight was a reassertion of innate individualism, or of trading habits become fixed through generations, or of a desire for more rapid advancement, or of dissatisfaction with a life of manual labor—whatever motivation, good or not so good, is ascribed to it—the fact is that in a society that glorified the middle class, the Jewish immigrant population had begun its ascent into that class. If so much is to be explained on the basis of folk habit, one must attribute to Jewish character also the interest that the second generation displayed in so-called white-collar occupations. Immigrant parents made every effort and sacrifice to send their children to high school and, if possible, college. The highest goal—even higher than that of business—was law or medicine for a son and teaching or, at least, secretarial work for a daughter. As Jews, having overcome great obstacles, sought to enter new and more respected economic areas, whether business or professional, they encountered new—in Jewish experience old—obstacles placed in their way by non-Jews already established in these areas.

2. THE TIDE OF ANTI-SEMITISM

There was a moment during the nineteenth century when the Jews of Europe were justified in looking forward hopefully to the disappearance of anti-Jewishness. The moment proved all too brief. When, during the Age of Rationalism, it became no longer fashionable to hate Jews for religious reasons, the racial reason, that is, anti-Semitism, was substituted. It proved even more serviceable than old-fashioned Jew-hatred as an excuse for condemning and hating Jews, since it is possible for a person to change his religion but quite impossible, according to the scientific theories of that day, to change one's racial character. The German-speaking countries, where Jews were making spectacular economic and, therefore, social progress, became the homeland of the

anti-Semites. In France, toward the end of the nineteenth
century, anti-Semitism played a crucial role in the political
upheaval known as the Dreyfus affair. The forces of liberal-
ism triumphed after six years of bitter conflict that showed
at every turn how deeply ingrained in the minds of the people was the dislike of Jews. Britain, with the broad sense of
fairness and tolerance that had become characteristic of it,
had abolished, some forty years before the end of the century, the last disabilities that had been imposed on the Jews.
Nevertheless, the anti-immigration movement at the beginning of the new century had about it a slight odor of anti-
Semistim. The Scandinavian countries, and Italy as well,
were almost completely free from this spiritual blight. Russia and Rumania, of course, provided an entirely different
case.

A considerable anti-Semitic literature, mostly in German,
circulated in Europe around the turn of the century. The
anti-Semites even banded themselves together in an international league, which met periodically for consultation and
propaganda. An occasional "ritual murder" scare, in various parts of the Austro-Hungarian empire, served to show
that religious prejudices were still prevalent among the
backward populations. The failure to permit Jews to become officers in the German army or to promote them to pro-
fessorships in German universities was also a holdover from
former days and could not be credited directly to the influence of the new anti-Semitism. Nevertheless, though it
seemed to show no practical results, anti-Semitism was planting, in the hearts of men, seeds that in time would bear their
poisonous fruit.

The Jews reacted with indignation and fear. Their ancestors barely a century before would have accepted these
spiritual aberrations of their neighbors as a matter of course:
being discriminated against was the price one paid for the
inner dignity and satisfaction of being a Jew. But the situation among the Jews at the beginning of the twentieth century differed in several respects from that of former days.

The Jews had understood emancipation to imply full acceptance into their respective nations. Also, they welcomed the rationalism of the age as insurance against prejudice. Above all, the end of official restrictions of movement, and the new cultural and economic opportunities, had brought larger numbers of Jews in direct contact with the non-Jewish world. In days gone by only a few outstandingly successful, or peripheral, Jews had had personal experience of rejection; the rest were submerged, or more or less accustomed to the existing situation, or had direct contacts only with neighbors. Now many more Jews experienced the physical pain and the emotional hurt of scorn, accusation, and rejection. They had to respond, to refute; and their response, dignified and intelligent enough, but perhaps for that very reason unpersuasive, took the form of issuing leaflets and books as counterpropaganda. Appeals to reason against an irrational emotion were bound to fail. Virtually every country in Europe had a defense organization to combat anti-Jewish propaganda and to guard against infringements of the rights of Jews. But the chief immediate result of revived anti-Jewishness was its effect on the Jews themselves. They became oversensitive and overcareful. A large measure of the opposition to Herzlian Zionism among the Jews of western Europe is traceable to the fear that sympathy with the rebuilding of the ancient land would be misinterpreted as lack of loyalty to a native or an adopted country.

Anti-Jewishness in the United States began differently and has given promise of ending differently, but some of the intermediate steps and some of the reactions on the part of Jews were not unlike those of Europe. European religious prejudices were imported with every group of settlers even in colonial days; under prevailing conditions, however, these prejudices could not thrive or have any lasting influence. When the national government came into being, it refused to recognize divisions according to religion; the Bill of Rights guaranteed the separation of Church and State. That there were occasional lapses into prejudice on the part of individuals must be taken for granted; but the attitude toward Jews on the part of the population as a whole must be set down as proof that where opportunities for economic betterment are plentiful and agitators scarce, the average sensible human being will not hold against his neighbor the fact that the latter differs from him in custom and religion. In the course of the nineteenth century, there were several occasions when the United States entered official protest, on humanitarian grounds, against mistreatment of Jews in foreign lands. It did so more vigorously when Jewish citizens of the United States were affected, not on the ground that the people maltreated were Jews, but on the ground that they were citizens, among whom the government of the United States made no distinctions because of religion. As late as 1887, President Grover Cleveland appointed a Jew, Oscar S. Straus, as minister to Turkey, in large measure in order to show prejudice-ridden Europeans that the United States did not practice discrimination. It can be said that the United States had grown to maturity as a nation without showing any substantial evidence of Old World anti-Jewishness. Among the general population, however, prejudice showed signs of spreading as the new century opened.

Many factors contributed to this change of atmosphere. One historian attributes it to the growing economic distress of the farmers, especially in the Middle West, and to the rise of an American aristocracy. Agitators tried to persuade the former to accept the idea, borrowed from the anti-Semitism of Europe, that alleged Jewish control of finance lay at the bottom of all troubles; the charge was that the Jews controlled Wall Street. The self-appointed aristocrats, largely representative of the real financial power in the country, desired no intrusion into their ranks and looked with dismay at the climb of some Jews up the economic ladder. Such attitudes at the top seeped down quickly. The immigrants—their numbers, their manners, and the slums they were accused of creating—were blamed for the rising tide of anti-Jewish feeling. It was a persuasive explanation, and many among the older strata of Jews were also prepared to accept it. The hollowness of the argument was immediately apparent through the fact that the completely assimilated German Jews were at that time also not spared the pains of prejudice. Moreover, as the children of the Jewish immigrants, though all but indistinguishable from the rest of the American population, began looking for occupations in fields in which Jews were formerly not conspicuous, the number of Jews exposed to hostility and discrimination increased. Restrictions began to appear on every side: against Jews desiring to move into better neighborhoods, against those seeking admission to better or socially more recognized schools, against those seeking to enter the legal, medical, or engineering profession. Certain economic areas, like banking and heavy industry, were completely closed to Jews. Restrictive advertisements, whether by resorts or employers, became common.

The American Jews had no organization to combat this intangible yet real menace. They became as ill-at-ease and, therefore, as apologetic as the west European Jews. The natural outlet for their discomfort was the same type of protest and explanation. Rabbis from their pulpits refuted every possible charge; but their audiences were Jews. The papers read and published by the American Jewish Historical Society (founded in 1892) concentrated on the part played by Jews in the birth and growth of the nation; but they again reached only a small number of people, and these almost exclusively Jews.

The aftermath of an event that occurred in 1903 indicated that anti-Jewishness was not yet so deep-seated as many Jews feared. A pogrom in Kishinev—another symptom of the czarist government's desire to draw the attention of the people away from the reforms that Russia so desperately needed—organized by the government itself, resulted in about forty lives lost, some six hundred people injured, and much property destroyed. The civilized world was horrified.

Protest meetings were addressed not only by Jews but also by distinguished representatives of the Christian population both in Britain and in America; conscience appeared to be still alive. Another indication of the fact that anti-Jewish feeling was not yet deep among the Christian population of the United States was the warm participation of leading non-Jews in the celebration, in 1905, of the two hundred fiftieth anniversary of the arrival of the first Jews in North America—the same event of which the three hundredth anniversary was celebrated in 1954 and 1955.

Realizing that, on the whole, the American people were not hostile to Jews and that the United States government represented public opinion in its firm and unequivocal condemnation of persecution in foreign lands, some of the foremost American Jews were encouraged to implement suggestions that had been made in the Jewish press for the organization of a general committee to serve the same purposes as were served by similar bodies in western European countries. Such an organization had existed in the United States from 1859 to 1878. It was called the Board of Delegates of American Israelites and comprised representatives from a number of congregations. Its effectiveness was limited, for it did not speak with the authority of a united Jewish community and received no regular support. In time it drifted nearer to the Reform Jewish group and was merged with the Union of American Hebrew Congregations with the understanding that its work would be continued by a special committee of the latter organization. The fact was that, at the time of the Kishinev massacre, no organization existed in the United States that could appeal to the entire Jewish community for relief funds, or that could approach the government in the name of all the Jews of the United States to lodge with the Russian government a protest against the outrage of which it was guilty.

As a consequence of this situation, an *ad hoc* committee had to be set up to raise funds for the relief of the surviving victims of the Kishinev massacre and others that followed.

Happily, the leaders of this committee, which included such widely known and highly respected persons as Oscar S. Straus, Jacob H. Schiff, Cyrus L. Sulzberger, Louis Marshall, Adolph Lewisohn, and others of similar stature, enjoyed the confidence of American Jews generally, who responded generously to the appeal for contributions. The funds raised were transmitted to representative Jewish bodies in Russia, which also were raising money there, for application to the needs of the situation.

The fact that an *ad hoc* committee had to be formed to meet this crisis was another factor in convincing those Jews to whom one turned when emergencies arose that a permanent representative body was urgently needed. How such a body should be organized was the subject of prolonged and earnest debate at two conferences, held in New York City, of individuals selected because they were recognized as leaders in their respective communities. There was much difference of opinion as to the basis of organization, but there was no difference of opinion as to the need for such a general body. Mayer Sulzberger, who was in the chair, was instructed to appoint a committee of fifteen who would co-opt forty-five additional members to constitute the general committee; later the membership of the general committee was increased from sixty to seventy-five. On November 11, 1906, these men met and established the American Jewish Committee.

One of the first steps taken by the new organization was to deal with what actually constituted a civil disability for American Jews. This was the fact that the Russian Government refused admission to that country of Jews from the United States, regardless of the place of their birth. This policy was a flagrant violation of the Treaty of Commerce and Navigation concluded between the United States and Russia in 1832. The United States government had protested against the policy repeatedly for almost half a century. The American Jewish Committee began by approaching President Theodore Roosevelt and his successor, William H.

Taft; both regretfully replied that the United States government could not see its way clear to taking any action other than continuing its diplomatic protests. Following this unsatisfactory response, the American Jewish Committee decided to demand and to agitate for the abrogation of the treaty of 1832 on the ground that as long as it continued in force, the civil and political equality of American Jews as citizens of the United States was actually abridged under the laws of the land, of which treaties are a part. Resolutions requesting President Taft to take the steps prescribed in the treaty to bring about its abrogation were introduced in both the Senate and the House of Representatives. Representatives of the American Jewish Committee, accompanied by leaders of several other Jewish organizations, appeared before the appropriate committees of the Congress and argued in favor of the resolutions. The case was strengthened by the fact that the American Jewish Committee learned that the embargo against the admission of American citizens affected not only Jews but also Catholic priests and Protestant missionaries. Backed by an aroused public opinion, which was the more ready to support the breaking of this bond with Russia because of the recent pogroms, the House of Representatives passed the abrogation resolution by a vote of three hundred to one; before the Senate was ready to consider this measure, President Taft notified that body that he, through diplomatic channels, had given the Russian government the year's notice of abrogation required by the treaty. The Senate thereupon adopted a resolution approving the President's action.

It was a victory that pleased Jews and reaffirmed the American guarantee of political equality. As was expected, it had no effect whatever on Russia. Two years later, Russia offered the world the spectacle of a thoroughly medieval "ritual murder" trial. In 1911 a Jew named Mendel Beilis had been arrested on the trumped-up charge of having killed a Christian child for purposes of the Jewish religion. The real culprit, the mother of the dead child, was easily identifiable; but despite the protests of liberal Russians and of groups of leaders in many western countries who ridiculed the "ritual murder" fable, the Russian government openly went to great lengths to have the Jew, and through him all Jews, convicted. The plot failed, not because of the protests and other expressions of disgust of the civilized part of the world, but because there simply was no evidence.

3. ZIONISM UNDER HERZL

It is not surprising that much of the Jewish population of the Russian empire was eager to escape from such an atmosphere and such pressures. What calls for explanation is why the vast majority chose to stay or hoped to go elsewhere than to the countries in which they or their children could expect material improvement. The explanation lies in their spiritually satisfying life. The inner life of the Jews of eastern Europe was now, in the decade preceding World War I, more active than ever. It was also more varied. One cannot divide a population into clear-cut segments, but groupings, with a great deal of overlapping, could be discerned among the Russian Jews of that day. The largest group maintained, deepened, and purified the characteristic east European Jewish religious life, both Hasidic and non-Hasidic. Such people were suspicious of the newly-formed diasporas, already notorious, as far as they were concerned, for their religious laxness, if not outright godlessness. Such Jews migrated only when their personal situations became quite intolerable or when family ties drew them to the distant land. At the other extreme, was a group whose hopes were centered in Russia's coming revolution. For there was a growing number of western-educated and increasingly assimilated Jews who felt that Russia could not long postpone democratization. Rather close to the latter were the workers and intellectuals who formed the backbone of the socialist, revolutionary, Yiddishist town dwellers of the Pale. Between the two extremes were those whose views, whether inclining more to the religious or more to the socialistic, were mingled with a sense of Jewish nationalism; whose cultural interests, though broad, were drawn to Hebrew as their language; whose humanist sentiments, though inclusive, could be traced back to the Bible and other sources of idealism, and were connected closely with the highly productive Hebrew and Yiddish literatures of the day. The usual centers of migration did not attract these Jews, being considered by them culturally barren. This group constituted the body and the hope of the Zionist movement.

There was a sense of urgency about Dr. Herzl's activity in behalf of the cause he represented, almost as though he knew how short his life would be. His visits to the Sultan and the Kaiser, to Russian diplomats and British statesmen, to wealthy Jews and influential Christians; his correspondence, the institutions he saw established to further the movement's aims, his arguments and negotiations before, at, and after the Zionist congresses—all testify to the intensity of his desire to achieve the Zionist aim in the shortest possible time. His almost feverish activity indicated his obsession by the idea; but it indicated also his conviction that Russian Jewry, perhaps European Jewry, and possibly, even world Jewry, had to be saved at once or the Jewish people would perish. It was a conviction touched with prophecy. Quite as prophetic was his description, in his *Altneuland,* of the progressive, efficient, modern Jewish state that would be in existence fifty years later. The two prophecies were joined in his mind, as they were destined to be joined in fact.

Herzl wanted to save the Russian Jews, who, all objective observers agreed, had to abandon the empire of the czar. With anti-Semitism almost everywhere in evidence, the best solution of the so-called Jewish question clearly was a homeland of their own for the Jewish people. But despite half a dozen years of active contact with some of the best among the Jewish people, Herzl, with his assimilationist background and inadequate Jewish upbringing, still did not realize the depth of Jewish attachment to Palestine. When the British government suggested Uganda in Africa as a place where a semi-independent Jewish community could be established, Herzl decided to place before the World Zionist Congress about to meet, in 1903, the proposal that the British offer of Uganda be accepted as a *Nacht-Asyl,* a temporary asylum. He was shocked by the effect the suggestion produced on the delegates representing the very Russian Jews he was so anxious to save. They viewed it as an abandonment of their dearest hopes, a betrayal. They would not hear of Uganda or of any other temporary asylum, but only of Palestine. The compromise arrived at, namely, to send an investigating commission, was merely a cover-up for a retreat from the entire scheme. It was to be Palestine, the ancient homeland, or nothing.

A number of Zionists, on the other hand, considered this stand quite unrealistic. Israel Zangwill, for example, noting the rising tide of objections to Jewish immigration to his native England, and to America, and fearful of the effects of assimilation on the future of the Jewish people, felt that a quicker solution had to be found than the one Zionism offered under its self-limitation to Palestine. The Jews, he argued, could not wait until the Sultan was persuaded to grant the charter to Palestine upon which Zionist hopes were based. Zangwill, therefore, seceded from the Zionist organization and founded the Jewish Territorial Organization (ITO), which looked for a Jewish home, or Jewish homes, wherever it or they could be found. He had to admit eventually that his apparently easier task proved at least as difficult; he was still searching for other homes when Zionism began taking giant steps forward.

Another aspect of the east European view of Zionism was a source of surprise to Herzl. He was impatient of the method of slow colonization the Hovevei Tsiyon had been pursuing for the quarter century before. Given to thinking in political terms, he considered colonization the wrong way to begin. The proper first step was to obtain a charter from the Sultan guaranteeing Jewish autonomy within the Turkish Empire. Admittedly, he was not getting far in that direction. That was why he tried to use the influence of the Kaiser and to bring whatever other pressure he could on the wary Abdul Hamid. Once the charter was obtained, he believed, the Jewish masses would flow into the land and rebuild it and their Judaism with it. He was astonished to find a substantial number of Zionists, mostly east Europeans, taking quite the opposite view. They considered the people's culture more basic than any political arrangements. We have seen that Ahad Ha'Am (Asher Ginzberg), the foremost interpreter of the Jewish spirit of that day, as well as all the other participants in the stirring revival of Hebrew culture, were more concerned with the people than with the land or with national autonomy. Chaim Weizmann, then a young scientist, was among the leaders of the opposition to Herzl.

Opposition, disappointment, ceaseless labor, destroyed Herzl. He died at the age of forty-four. Everyone, the east European Jews most of all, recognized that the cause had lost its great leader. Everyone feared that Zionism would collapse. But it went on, though without the drive of Herzl's personality and his resourcefulness. David Wolffsohn, Herzl's successor in the presidency of the World Zionist Organization, was a mild-mannered businessman who had all he could do to keep things going. Yet the organization and the institutions that Herzl had founded continued to function. The work for a charter and the other political plans were now relegated to second place. The opposition had triumphed in a way it certainly had not wished, but the fact was that it had the field practically to itself. Palestine was to be built through agricultural settlements and cultural renaissance.

Two ideals motivated the young people whose arrival in Palestine between 1904 and the outbreak of World War I is designated the Second Aliyah ("ascent"): the ideal of reviving the Jewish nation on its ancestral soil and the ideal of socialism, which they understood to mean a nonexploiting society. They objected to the employment of Arabs, because for one thing, this would limit the opportunities for Jewish immigration, and perhaps more important, it would turn the Jews into supervisors of a peasant Arab population. Their views found expression in the personality and writings of the remarkable A. D. Gordon (1856-1922). Arriving in Palestine in 1904, at the age of forty-eight, he insisted on becoming a common laborer. He evolved the principle of "the Conquest of Labor," indeed, the holiness of labor. Fortunately, too, the World Zionist Organization established a labor office in Palestine in charge of the wise and gifted Dr. Arthur Ruppin (1876-1942). Moreover, the Organization soon succeeded in persuading the new Turkish government (1908) to permit the acquisition of land by Jews. The newly-established *Keren Kayyemet* (Jewish National Fund) became the purchasing and holding agency of the national soil, to which it retained title but which it let the colonists work. Thus a number of colonies were founded in every part of the country. They were soon to take various forms: collectivist, both economically and socially, co-operative, or individual in ownership. Not all the problems were solved, but the entire Zionist enterprise began to take shape and give promise.

There were other significant developments, during this brief decade and a half, testifying to the creative vitality of the *Yishuv* (the Jewish-settled community in Palestine). The organization of the *shomerim,* a band of Jewish armed guards, to protect the colonies from nocturnal incursions of Arabs bent on theft, lent an air of frontier romance to the history of the period. The foundation of Tel Aviv, a new suburb on the sandy outskirts of Jaffa, which a few years later was to mushroom into a city, was another foreshadowing of the future. As important as any manifestation of vitality was the emergence of Hebrew as an everyday, spoken language. Poets and publicists and novelists had been urging such a development for a century, not without some bitterness against Yiddish, which they identified with exile and spiritual subservience. What could not be achieved by arguments and pleas in the larger centers of eastern Europe, the tiny but ardent settlement in Palestine willed into existence.

The process had begun in the days of the First Aliyah. It seemed natural for those who came to revive the ancient land to desire to revive its ancient language. They adopted Sephardic pronunciation, modifying it slightly, ostensibly because they persuaded themselves that the language had been spoken thus in ancient times. In all likelihood, there was here, too, the subconscious motivation of wanting to break with the exile, the ghetto, and all that it had brought into Jewish life. The Second Aliyah fortified the earlier decision to bring the Hebrew language to life. In the schools that were established the children were taught in Hebrew only. Unfortunately, the classical Hebrew that was available did not suffice for the modernity that was equally a part of the new *Yishuv's* heritage. Now, however, the influence of Eliezer ben Yehudah began to be felt. A man of indomitable spirit, he made the speaking of Hebrew a principle of life with which he brooked no compromise. If the Hebrew vocabulary was inadequate, he single-handedly undertook to enlarge it. In his many-volumed dictionary, he drew upon Arabic and he Hebraized western terms. Later Hebraists changed many of his locutions, but he had laid the foundations of the revived language.

The intense loyalty the *Yishuv* had begun to feel to the Hebrew language came to the surface when the community thought it was being threatened or even slighted. The Hilfsverein der deutschen Juden opened a technical school in Haifa. Arguing that Hebrew was not yet ripe for effective use in scientific studies, the directors announced that the school would use German in the technical courses. At once, pupils and teachers went on strike. It is by no means certain to this day that the German directors wanted to sidetrack Hebrew, but they had obviously touched a very sensitive nerve in the spirit of the community. The long and heated argument had the effect of making the World Zionist Organization take on educational functions along with its other activities. Above all, the struggle made it perfectly clear that Hebrew was to be the language of the future among the Jews of Palestine.

The *Yishuv* was thus taking firm root. Years of development still lay ahead, hard struggles in every sphere; but there was every reason to expect that in the course of some generations, a healthy community would grow and prosper. Suddenly, a world-shaking tragedy loomed out of the west and threatened to destroy all that had been achieved. Yet out of that tragedy came the unexpected—that charter recognizing Jewish rights in Palestine for which Herzl had worked and because of which he had been derided and opposed. This, however, is a story so closely connected with the western diaspora that attention must once more be centered there.

4. VARIETIES OF JUDAISM AND EXPERIMENTS IN UNITY

It had been Ahad Ha'Am's contention from the very beginning that what the Jews were experiencing was a crisis of Judaism rather than a crisis of the Jewish people. Total and ignominious assimilation, he maintained, was a greater and more imminent danger than anti-Semitism in the west and persecution in the east. Both Herzlian Zionists and the defense organizations that had grown up in the various countries of western Europe put the solution of social and political problems first. The advocates of strengthening the Jewishness of Jewish life in the western communities were indeed numerous and sometimes vociferous, but hopelessly divided as to aims and means.

Religion, more than any other aspect of Jewish life, revealed the wide divisions that existed among Jews. In Germany advocates of greater Reform organized a union in 1908, and extreme Orthodoxy countered by establishing a world union of its own under the name of Agudath Yisroel (1912). In France the consistorial system (1905) aimed to unify French Jewry on a religious-communal basis, but that did not prevent the east European immigrants from establishing synagogues quite independent of the consistory. At the same time a Reform movement appeared and also established a synagogue in Paris. In England, where Judaism had a long tradition of unity because of the official and unofficial functioning of the United Synagogue and its Chief Rabbinate, there came into being an Orthodox *Kehilla* on the Frankfort-German model, a federation of synagogues of the east European type, as well as a Liberal synagogue taking its cue from American Reform Judaism.

Nowhere was religious division more apparent and more articulate than in the United States. The emergence of three distinct religious viewpoints by the beginning of the twentieth century has already been mentioned. Of the three, the Reform group alone was well-organized. The Union of American Hebrew Congregations was a flourishing body; Isaac M. Wise had given it extraordinary leadership. On his death (1900) the presidency of the Hebrew Union College eventually went to Kaufmann Kohler (1903), scholar and theologian. Reform might soon have become the dominant religious view of American Judaism had it not been characterized during that crucial decade by religious radicalism, social exclusiveness, and anti-Zionism. Orthodox Jewry had, indeed, made a feeble effort at strength through union when, in 1888, it had invited Rabbi Jacob Joseph of Vilna to become the chief rabbi of the Russian Jewish congregations in New York. The plan failed completely. The chief rabbi's authority was flouted by his colleagues and not supported by laymen. At his death (1902) the situation reverted to chaos. The Union of Orthodox Jewish Congregations, which had been organized in 1898, proved far too weak. No area of Jewish life, from *kashrut* to education, was given the necessary supervision. The congregations were not only independent of one another but also antagonistic to each other. The Yeshivah (the Rabbi Isaac Elhanan Theological Seminary, organized in 1896) enjoyed but minor status when European-trained rabbis were readily available. Not till

1915, with the appointment to its presidency of Bernard Revel (1885-1940), did the institution begin to exert influence on American Orthodoxy.

The Jewish Theological Seminary had been marking time since the death of Sabato Morais (1897). The institution's appeal to Americanized traditionalist Jews, by and for whom it had been founded, had never been either vigorous or effective. Its sole contribution had been the preparation of a number of scholarly rabbis who could preach in English to congregations that still maintained the Orthodox ritual. The entire situation changed with the coming to the Seminary's presidency of Solomon Schechter. He was a scholar and a sage, a brilliant writer, and an ardent fighter in behalf of a living, functioning, traditional Judaism. Behind him stood some of the finest spirits in American Israel, Jacob H. Schiff and Louis Marshall, though themselves identified with a Reform congregation, Cyrus Adler and Solomon Solis-Cohen who had been brought up in the Sephardic congregation of Leeser and Morais, and many other important individuals, though comparatively few congregations. Dr. Schechter set forth his goal for American Judaism as organized traditionalism grounded in learning. He began to build on the model of the Breslau seminary founded by Zechariah Frankel in 1854. He invited first-rate young scholars like Louis Ginzberg, Alexander Marx, Israel Friedlaender, and Mordecai M. Kaplan to serve on the Seminary's faculty. He laid the foundation of what was to become, under the guidance of Professor Marx, one of the foremost Jewish libraries in the world. Under him, the Jewish Theological Seminary began to graduate rabbis who could challenge the leadership of the reformers. In 1913 Schechter founded the United Synagogue of America, dedicated to what he preferred to call Historical Judaism, but what has come to be known as Conservative Judaism.

All of these religious movements and institutions combined, it must be remembered, did not command the adherence of all the Jews in the United States, any more than similar movements and institutions claimed the loyalty of all in the countries of Europe. A very substantial minority of the newly-arrived immigrants, as well as of the older residents, was indifferent to affiliation with organized religion of any kind. This reflected the trend, noticeable, among Protestants more than among Catholics, in the general population. That lack of affiliation was more apparent in the Jewish group may be accounted for by a number of considerations: the impression that adjustment demanded the obliteration of all differences, the special susceptibility to rationalist influences on the part of the westernized Jews of that day, the inability of immigrant parents to transmit their heritage in the terms of their new environment, and finally, the patent fact that Jews can express their Jewishness in ways other than public or even private worship. Each of the numerous organizations that claimed the loyalty of Jews— B'nai B'rith lodges, *landsmanshaften,* the Workmen's Circle, Zionist Clubs, and any number of other groups of a philanthropic nature—could claim to be an expression of the Jewish spirit.

This fragmentation of Jewish life may have made it colorful and interesting, but it also made it chaotic. Disorganization of Jewish life had long troubled some of those who stood at its forefront, but it took an ugly incident to stir them to action. In 1908, the police commissioner of New York City published an article in which he voiced current anti-immigrant prejudices by saying that half the city's criminals were Jews. In the face of a storm of protest, the commissioner retracted the ill-advised and easily-disproved accusation. But the incident showed how important it was for the Jews to draw together in defense of their common interests. Judah L. Magnes, already a powerful influence in American Jewish life—and, though at the time rabbi of the Reform Temple Emanu-El, loved by the Jews of the lower East Side of New York—decided that it was time to act. Characteristically, he was concerned not so much with defending the good name of the Jews as with bringing to the fore their latent spiritual qualities. The Jews of New York must organize on a democratic basis to deal with the variety of problems that confronted them. Thus, in February 1909, the New York *Kehilla* came into existence.

The name of the city-wide organization was reminiscent of the *Kahal,* the official Jewish community that had functioned for many centuries in every town in Europe. The new body itself was in effect quite different from the old *Kahal.* It consisted of representatives, based on membership, of every variety of Jewish organization—synagogue, lodge, philanthropy, and all the rest. The "downtowners" were there and the "uptowners" too, for Magnes sought to tie the American Jewish Committee, be it ever so loosely, to the Jewish efforts for internal unity. The aims were as broad as Magnes's hopes were high: "Nothing Jewish should be foreign to the Jewish community of New York." It was going to institute supervision of *kashrut,* to improve Jewish education, to gather statistics in various areas of Jewish life, to strengthen and democratize philanthropy, and to participate in any number of other activities. There was great enthusiasm, which carried over to other cities. A similar *Kehilla* was actually formed in Philadelphia, and there was talk about the formation of such organizations in other cities as well.

Yet the glowing hopes came to little. After the first year or two, enthusiasm waned. Magnes's popularity kept it going for almost a decade, but by 1918 it petered out completely. The reasons for its demise were inherent in the Jewish population and in Magnes. Jews among themselves had not yet overcome suspicions and prejudices based on their places of origin. Too may toes were being stepped on in the plans for various kinds of supervision. There was still too much antagonism between the socially and economically distinct portions of the city's Jewish inhabitants. The intellectual differences could not be bridged. Above all, World War I broke out, and interest was diverted to the tragic plight of the Jews in Europe. Magnes himself, courageous and outspokenly idealistic, moved against the current of American sentiment with regard both to the War and to the revolutionary events in Russia, and so fell under a cloud. Losing him, the *Kehilla* lost its vital spirit and ceased to function.

Nevertheless, all was not lost. The *Kehilla* of New York left a legacy in the form of several institutions that continued to exert a constructive influence on Jewish life. Among these, a school for Jewish social workers functioned for a number of years. There was, above all, the Bureau of Jewish Education, which soon began a fruitful career under the direction of Samson Benderly (1876-1944). He brought system into the organization, and method into the conduct of the Jewish school. He surrounded himself with promising young college men whom he inspired to make Jewish education their life work. By persuading several important schools to pay their teachers a living wage, he raised the prestige of the Jewish teaching profession. By encouraging the preparation of new textbooks and urging the adoption of Hebrew as the language of instruction, he brought new spirit into the child's introduction to Jewish life. His cause was aided by the arrival in the United States of a number of excellent teachers as well as by the inspiration deriving from Zionist thought. Through the Bureau, Benderly, aided by a substantial fund given by Jacob H. Schiff, knew how to translate all this into program and curriculum. Before long, many of the larger Jewish communities made serious efforts to co-ordinate their schools through similar bureaus of Jewish education.

The *Kehilla,* despite its failure, proved that forces making for broad unity were stirring within the Jewish population. Actual co-operation during days of peace and for the difficult purpose of inner reconstruction required more self-effacement than was as yet possible; too many memories and too many prejudices still divided group from group. But already a generation was growing up in whose spirit a common upbringing was to outweigh the divisive influences of the past.

Moreover, even before that generation came into its own, a challenge hurled at the Jewries of the west, especially that of America, compelled them to assume responsibilities from which they would ordinarily have shrunk as beyond their powers.

III

. . . .

War and Its Consequences

. . . .

1. BETWEEN TWO FIRES

It has been pointed out often that in time of war Jews suffer in double measure: as part of the embattled nations and as Jews. Every army in World War I had its Jewish soldiers, usually in a ratio higher than the proportion of Jews in the nation's population. By accusing the Jews of being shirkers, anti-Semites succeeded in proving the high scale of Jewish participation. For several governments, among them both the German and the Russian, undertook to investigate the accusation, and to their surprise, came up with astonishingly high figures. Tens of thousands of Jewish soldiers met death on the battlefields, and an unusually large number of Jews in every army was cited for bravery.

Anti-Semites usually lie low during periods of actual fighting. In the lands of the czar, however, official anti-Jewishness was quite as rampant as in time of peace. Since most of the fighting was done in the western provinces of the empire, which coincided for the most part with the Pale of Jewish Settlement, the Jewish civil population was in almost greater danger than the fighting forces. Many Jews were ruthlessly uprooted on suspicion that they would side with the enemy. The fact that the commanders of German occupation forces, in one or another province, dealt kindly with the Jews in order to win their support was sufficient for the Russians to accuse the Jews of collaborating with the enemy. When a city was won back by the Russians, the Jews paid heavily for the comparative quiet they had enjoyed under German occupation. Throughout the war the Jews of eastern Europe suffered every misery.

The war's end was even worse. The havoc of war was followed by the horrors of revolution. The democratic Kerensky government, which replaced the czar, and which Jews the world over hailed with delight, was soon overthrown by the Bolsheviks. A double war began. On the one hand, there were the forces of reaction; moving across the Ukraine, they organized anti-Jewish pogroms in every town they captured or were about to evacuate. On the other hand, there was the ruthless communist policy of exterminating the middle class, in which the Jews were largely represented. Religious observance, devotion to Jewish studies, to Zionism, to the Hebrew language—all were pronounced counterrevolutionary, and punished with Siberian exile, if not death. To be sure, the communists took an official stand against pogroms, but this stand was largely theoretical in view of the chaotic conditions. On balance, the cure for czarism was as bad as the disease.

The cries of distress that reached the Jews of the more fortunately situated west, from the beginning of the war and long beyond its end, touched the heartstrings of all who heard them, especially the Jews of America. Three national relief committees were organized almost at once to meet the situation. Before long they joined in a single body under the chairmanship of Felix M. Warburg (1871-1937). The American Joint Distribution Committee for the Relief of Jewish War Sufferers, soon to be known in Europe as "The Joint" and in America as the JDC, began to distribute the funds raised by the relief committees in what would before then have been considered incredible amounts. The efficiency of the distribution equaled that of the collection. There were even martyrs connected with the transmission of the funds to the Jews of the eastern provinces: Professor Israel Friedlaender and Rabbi Bernard Cantor, while on their mission of relief in eastern Ukraine, were shot down by a band of Ukrainian marauders (1920). Without the funds gathered with such devotion and distributed at such risk, it is certain that scores of thousands would have succumbed. But, as far as the Jews of the United States were concerned, the war emergency had a result of an entirely different kind, which astonished them more than anyone else. It showed them ready to meet a challenge, willing to shoulder responsibility, and capable of a degree of co-operation that gave promise of a brighter communal future.

2. PROMISE AND RETRACTION

In addition to the war problems of eastern Europe, danger threatened the Jewish community of Palestine. Some 85,000 Jews were living there when the War broke out, half of them immigrants of the First and Second Aliyot. Many of the younger Jews were forced into the Turkish army; others fled. Suspecting its sympathies with the Allies, the Turkish commander decreed the destruction of the entire Jewish settlement. Henry Morgenthau, the United States ambassador to Turkey, transmitted a warning of the danger, and the Jews of the United States through President Woodrow Wilson, as well as the Jews of Germany through their government, did what they could to stay the execution of the threat. American Jews came to the rescue. Jacob H. Schiff and the American Jewish Committee joined the Zionist Organization of America in sending the sum of $50,000 to Mr. Morgenthau. Other forces were also at work, so that at the very moment when the situation appeared exceedingly dark, it took a remarkable turn and began to bring the highest Zionist hopes nearer to realization.

The work of the World Zionist Organization was practically disrupted during the war years. Its leaders were scattered. Its task of building the Palestinian Jewish community had to yield to the labor of preventing the destruction of what had already been built. Chaim Weizmann was in England where, since 1903, he had been teaching chemistry at the University of Manchester and where, during the war years, he performed outstanding service for his adopted country. Shmarya Levin, a former member of the Russian Duma, and an extraordinarily effective Yiddish orator, had gone to the United States at the outbreak of war in Europe and kept Zionist interest alive among American Jews. At the same time, a new leader of American Zionism emerged in the statesmanlike Louis D. Brandeis (1856-1941), soon to be appointed by President Wilson to the United States Supreme Court (1916).

Early in the war, both the Allies and the Central Powers began to cast about for ways of gaining the sympathy of the world's population. Each side saw advantages in enlisting the support of Jews everywhere. Each side planned to promise that, as soon as practicable after the war, Palestine would be turned into a Jewish commonwealth. Germany could not as easily dispose of its Turkish partner's territory as could Britain and France of land belonging to their enemy. A great deal of secret negotiating was done with the Arabs, among the Allies themselves—soon to include the United States—as well as with leading Zionist and non-Zionist Jews. President Woodrow Wilson's sympathies were kept alive by Rabbi Stephen S. Wise and by Justice Louis D. Brandeis; their vision and idealism in the end outweighed the presumed "realism" of the Department of State. When it seemed likely that Britain's General Edmund Allenby would soon drive the Turks out of Palestine, the fateful announcement was made. On November 2, 1917, in a letter to Lord Rothschild, Arthur James Balfour, British Foreign Secretary, let it be known, on behalf of the British government, that the British "view with favor the establishment in Palestine of a national home for the Jewish people . . . it being clearly understood that nothing shall be done which may prejudice the civil and religious rights of existing non-Jewish communities in Palestine, or the rights and political status enjoyed by Jews in any other country." When, a few weeks later, on December 9, which corresponded to the first day of Hanukkah, Jerusalem actually fell to the British, it seemed to everyone that a new era of Jewish history had opened. On December 10, General Allenby made his entry into the city, where the Jews hailed him as their deliverer.

A great deal had to be done before the Balfour Declaration could assume reality. First, the war had to be won by the Allies. As an earnest of Jewish participation in the war, a battalion of some five thousand Jews, volunteers from Palestine and the United States, had been organized under Vladimir Jabotinsky; it arrived in Palestine in February

1918. Some months later, Galilee was occupied by the British; making it possible to extend the work of relief and reconstruction to the entire country. But before a civil government could be organized, through which the promise of a "home for the Jewish people" could be fulfilled, the transfer of Palestine to Britain, which had made the promise, had to be ratified by the Allied governments. A conference of these powers met at San Remo in April 1920 and gave the mandate over Palestine to Great Britain, charging it with the implementation of the Balfour Declaration. This action, in turn, was approved by the Council of the League of Nations in July 1922. It looked as though Herzl's dream of a charter, publicly recognized by the civilized world, had actually and miraculously come to pass.

But difficulties could and did arise. They began early. Zionist leaders, taking the Balfour Declaration very much in earnest, arrived in Palestine prepared to govern; and they immediately clashed with the British military government and with some civil servants who quite cynically looked upon the Declaration as merely a promise made under the pressures of war. The Arab upper class soon awoke to the fact that it still had a chance to gain control of the situation. The Arabs protested, and they organized riots. Their views prevailed so far that in 1922, even before the League of Nations had confirmed the mandate to Britain, Winston Churchill for the British government, in a letter to Chaim Weizmann, issued the first official interpretation of the Balfour Declaration, and watered it down considerably. It was explained to mean that the Jews could establish a community in Palestine—they were there "of right and not of sufferance"—but they could not consider it theirs in the sense of developing it as their own country.

This was a blow to Jewish expectations, the first of many that were to follow; but at the time, its full significance was lost upon the Jews preoccupied with building up the *Yishuv*. They were pleased with the appointment of Sir Herbert Samuel as the first high commissioner of Palestine (1920-

1925). They were pleased with the steady flow of idealistic, devoted, hard-working young people who came from eastern Europe as pioneers (*halutzim*) to build the Jewish home. New colonies, new institutions, new forces were created through the work of this, the Third Aliyah. Jews all over the world participated joyfully, as an indication of Jewish hope and character, in the establishment in this poor and struggling country of the Hebrew University on Mt. Scopus in Jerusalem. It was opened with dignified ceremonies in April 1925. Its first president was Dr. Judah L. Magnes.

3. MINORITY RIGHTS

Another situation that Jews met with vigor and imagination, thus turning tragedy into promise, was connected with their hope for reviving Jewish life in the war-stricken communities. For almost half a century the fate of the east European Jews had been uppermost in the minds of their western brothers. Whether as residents in, or emigrants from, the east European lands of oppression, these Jews had been a constant problem. Now the war had given this problem a new and more terrible twist. Immediate needs had been provided for by generosity; but what of the future? Could the Jews be left to the mercies of the new and the enlarged states being organized under ultranationalistic governments that might be worse than those of Russia and Rumania of the past? The Jews of the Allied lands began to wonder whether some permanent solution could not be found to guarantee the safety and future of the Jews in central and eastern Europe. They hoped to persuade the planners of peace not to overlook the fate of the Jews in the very countries where they were most numerous and most in need of protection.

As the time approached for the Paris Peace Conference, representative Jews came from the affected east European countries, excepting the new Russia, which was given no share in the peace negotiations. The Jews of England and France also sent representatives, picked without much difficulty from the outstanding personalities of the English and French Jewish communities. In the United States, however, there arose considerable discussion and conflict regarding the choice of delegates to this unofficial Jewish conference. The conflict must be touched upon, not only because it led to the establishment of an important organization in American Jewry, but also because it was, in a sense, a declaration of maturity on the part of a substantial portion of the Jewish population in the United States.

The American Jewish Committee, which since its establishment in 1906, had been dealing with the protection of the civil and religious rights of Jews in the United States and abroad, decided to send delegates to Paris. But there were objections to this assumption of authority, on the ground that although the membership of the Committee consisted of the most prominent men of every city, this membership was not elected by any local group. The charge, therefore, was that the Committee was undemocratically organized and could not be said properly to represent the Jews of the United States. Moreover, at the beginning of the century, when the Committee had come into being, Jewish leadership was in the hands primarily of German Jews; by 1918, however, the east European Jews, or their sons, had grown in wealth, status, and self-consciousness. Many of them had long been chafing under the assumption of leadership by the Jews of presumed German extraction. Finally, although there were Zionists in its membership, the American Jewish Committee's attitude toward Zionism was regarded as, at best, only lukewarm. Zionist leaders, considering the situation ripe for founding a representative body on democratic lines, formed a committee for the organization of an American Jewish Congress to consist of members elected by popular vote in each community. Opposition to the creation of such a representative body was expressed in some quarters, especially by the American Jewish Committee and other organizations, and a heated controversy ensued in the Jewish press. Another source of conflict was the announcement by the proponents of the Congress of their desire to demand of the eventual peace conference, not only equal political, civil, and religious rights for Jews, but also national rights for the Jews of eastern Europe.

After months of discussion and of negotiation between the leaders of both sides, a compromise was reached. The pro-Congress leaders agreed that the Congress when established should continue only until the task of its delegation to the peace conference was completed; the anti-Congress leaders agreed to the inclusion of a demand for what they insisted be called "group rights": wherever such "rights" were given to other groups of a population, they should be given to Jews as well. It was also agreed that, in addition to delegates to the Congress elected by popular vote, nationwide organizations (such as the B'nai B'rith and the American Jewish Committee) would also be given representation.

The delegations of the various Jewish communities assembled in Paris represented the majority of the Jews of the world. They soon decided to join forces and thereby strengthen their influence, especially if they could decide on common objectives. They therefore organized themselves as the Committee of Jewish Delegations at the Peace Conference. The westerners recognized before long that such principles as equality before the law, and the rights of citizenship, which were part and parcel of the western form of democracy, did not completely correspond to the needs of the Jews of eastern Europe. The latter felt that there were aspects of Jewish life that they were as eager to preserve as they were to gain their rights as citizens and that, they were sure, the majority of their non-Jewish neighbors would try to sabotage.

It thus came about that a new principle, to be known as Minority Rights, was accepted in international law. It was written into the peace treaties made with Austria, Hungary, Bulgaria, and Turkey. Special treaties on the subject were signed with Poland, Czechoslovakia, Yugoslavia, Rumania, and Greece. Still other states, like Latvia and Lithuania, which now regained their independence after centuries of foreign rule, issued special declarations affirming the new principle. The rights it guaranteed applied not only to Jews, but to all "racial, linguistic and religious minorities" that wanted to take advantage of them (only in the cases of Poland and Rumania, were Jews mentioned specifically). It meant that members of a minority were within their rights, if they so desired, in using their own language, conducting their own schools, living under their own religious laws, and organizing their own communities. They could do all this without being looked upon as alien to the state of which they were a part and whose citizenship they were entitled to possess. In educational matters, a minority had a right to an equitable share of state funds. Thus no majority could destroy a minority's culture under the specious argument of wanting a unified state. The system worked well in some countries for a number of years; it would have continued to do so had the League of Nations had the power to preserve it against just that type of blind nationalism and racialism which the Jews foresaw and against which the minority rights were meant to serve as a protection.

The first twenty years of the twentieth century appear in retrospect to have been a highly productive period in the life of the Jewish people. The challenges had been many and some of them had gone to the very roots of Jewish life; but the responses to them had been fruitful, or at least, promising. Little has been said so far about the area of culture and religion, for here developments during this period proved to have been inconclusive; moreover, the story of Judaism must be told in unbroken sequence and must therefore be deferred. In other areas of life, however, Jews faced up to every problem. Their attempts to solve them may not have brought lasting results, but even so, they showed the strength and resilience of the Jewish spirit. The desire to speed the absorption of the immigrants had resulted in the establishment of social and charitable institutions that eventually benefited the total community. The American Jewish Committee's stand in defending the rights of American Jewish citizens against the prejudices of Russian czarism, was to be a victory not for the Jews, but for American dignity. Jewish labor unions had helped develop some novel methods of co-operation with management. The threat to the physical and cultural survival of the Jews in eastern Europe, apart from evoking an unprecedented philanthropic response, had set in motion a new experiment in the international protection of minorities. The opportunity to build a national home had resulted in an enthusiastic flow of pioneers and in a first act toward the fulfillment of the Zionist aim. If some of these responses to the problems that had faced Jews proved ephemeral, it was because western civilization failed to be equally creative in meeting the forces that challenged it.

IV

. . . .

Two Decades of Retrogression

. . . .

1. CONTRIBUTORS AND INTERPRETERS

One aspect of Jewish experience during the first half of the twentieth century was the relationship between the Jews and western culture. The story of this relationship, almost more than anything else, makes one realize the extent to which Jewish life and thought, in a process which became most apparent during the 1920's, was revolutionized. Western and central European Jews had long been taking advantage of the cultural opportunities that a more tolerant and optimistic world offered them. Now larger numbers of east European Jews began enjoying contact with the novel, intellectually and spiritually stimulating environment. Unfortunately the broad-mindedness with which the century opened did not long survive World War I. It is instructive to see how the Jews responded to the warm and inviting cultural climate at the beginning of the century and how their spirits were affected when, in its third and fourth decades, that climate changed.

Literature offers the best means of studying the extent and effect of these cultural events. As the twentieth century opened there was hardly an important European literature to which the Jews were not contributing. Theodor Herzl, as journalist and dramatist, was but one example of a Jew who rose high in the general culture of his day. Two of his colleagues in the Zionist movement were equally noted in their respective countries and areas of activity: Israel Zangwill (1864-1926) as a dramatist in England, and Max Nordau (Budapest 1849-Paris 1923), whose books were among the best sellers of his day in every European langauge, as social critic and essayist in France. Perhaps the best example for the period at the turn of the century was Georg Brandes (1842-1927), who though born George Morris Cohen, evinced practically no interest in anything Jewish, while his widely read and applauded *Main Currents of Literature in the Nineteenth Century* (1872-5; English translation 1901-5) showed deep understanding of western culture.

Arthur Schnitzler, Ernst Toller, Jacob Wassermann, Franz Werfel, Arnold and Stefan Zweig were some of the men whose writings were translated into every civilized tongue, whose words and thoughts echoed the profoundest yearnings of the human spirit. Their patriotism was directed to the best in their respective fatherlands, and above that, to all that was human and universal in civilization. They were the "good Europeans" about whom so much was said. They knew, of course, that the dominant national cultures in whose midst they lived had a terrifying aspect too, one that expressed itself in chauvinism and militarism, in arrogance and prejudice. They fought this ugliness as long as they could, but it ultimately triumphed over them. Then, in the 1930's, their countries scorned and repudiated the labors of these representatives of Europeanism, drove them into exile, and burned their books.

Jews and Judaism figured but rarely in the writings of these Jewish men of letters. When Jews were introduced in their stories they were described in terms that might characterize the authors themselves: Jews by birth; aware of their Jewish heritage, but not nearly as interested in or hopeful about Judaism's future development as they were concerned with the development of the general culture. Fearful of their non-Jewish neighbors, sometimes even disdainful of the official hypocrisy about them, they nevertheless were eager to be absorbed into the majority. A writer of historical fiction like Lion Feuchtwanger repeatedly portrayed the Jew's contribution to European society as that of a shrewd advisor, a tamer of savagery, but an eventual scapegoat. On a different level, but suggesting similar overtones of pessimism, Richard Beer-Hofmann tried to interpret and justify the Jewish situation in messianic terms when, in his poetic drama *Jacob's Dream,* he explained Israel's hopes and suffering by evoking the mission that Father Jacob had accepted as his descendants' role in history.

No one reflected the ambivalence of the westernized Jew better than Franz Kafka (1883-1924), the German-writing

Czech Jew who was to have so much influence on the ill-adjusted generation that followed. His jottings, diaries, and personal letters occasionally show an interest in Jews and Judaism the existence of which one might never have guessed from his more formal writings. He seems to have been fascinated by the subject of his Jewishness and at the same time repelled by it. He dabbled for brief periods in Zionism and anti-Zionism; he tried to study Hebrew; he even looked into Hasidism. Yet he remained an admirer of the non-Jews and of the non-Jewish world, despite his resentment of its ubiquitous anti-Semitism. It is pointless to ask whether any Jewish influence is perceptible in Kafka's writing or in that of his like-minded contemporaries. Any answer has been, as it must be, a subjective one. The fact is, that even though these authors shared the Jewish fate, they gave scant expression in their writings to Jewish hopes and strivings.

There were, however, among the Jews of those decades two literary currents about whose Jewish nature there could be no doubt. The flowering Yiddish literature was one; the growing and developing Hebrew literature was the other. Both were now drawing their inspiration in large part from the literary and cultural currents on which all western literature lived. The generation following Mendele and Shalom Aleichem was no longer interested in reforming Jewish communal and social life; its writers considered themselves artists, not preachers. They were not even nostalgic seekers after the beauties of the Jewish spirit, as Peretz had been. They were proud realists, and this to them meant portraying the Jew and his fate in somber colors. They stood for rationalism with regard to the Jewish religion, for cosmopolitanism with regard to the Jewish people, and for pessimism with regard to the Jewish future.

To a greater or lesser extent the same attitude characterized each of the three groups into which Yiddish writers became divided after World War I, when the Russian-Polish center of Jewish life was broken up as a result of war and revolution into three centers, Russian, Polish, and American, each of which reflected its own cultural and political environment. The Soviet group, of necessity, articulated only one viewpoint—antireligious, non-Hebraic, hostile to Zionism, and submissive to communism. Its poets and novelists glorified the revolution and spoke glowingly of Jewish participation in the building of a new Russia. Yet they could not but hint at the tragedy of the starving Jewish spirit. Perhaps this is why the new anti-Jewishness that swept over Russia beginning with the early 1950's led to the death of the few remaining Jewish men of letters.

Polish Jewry, down to its liquidation by the Nazis, continued its extensive literary activity. A large Jewish population, steeped in Jewish tradition, and by the time of World War I, already possessed of considerable general culture, was bound to produce a rich literature. It used the Yiddish language and dealt with Jews, but was no more parochial than any other literature. The writings of Polish Jewish authors, both those living in Poland and those who migrated to western Europe and the United States, could stand comparison with whatever the non-Jewish Poles had to offer. Being creative artists, the Jewish authors could not but reflect in their works the bleak and ominous conditions under which the Jews of Poland lived. This, added to the spiritual chaos in some important Jewish circles, resulted in a literature largely dominated by a sense of doom and disintegration. There was no question here of the self-hate that appeared in some American Jewish writing of the 1930's and later; it was rather a case of realism not unmixed with pity and understanding.

The broad humanitarianism of this literature, and its ability to connect Jewish fate with the fate of the western world are best exemplified in a number of novels that were, translated into English and widely read: I. J. Singer's *The Brothers Ashkenazi*, Isaac Bashevis Singer's *The Family Moskat*—written after World War II but reflecting prewar

Jewish life—and Sholem Asch's *Three Cities*. These novels certainly did not idealize their Jewish characters. On the background of a world fast sinking into savagery, the Jewish authors indicated the spiritual emptiness of those who had adopted an alien way of life, an alien set of values.

But this was not all; the Yiddish writers were not content merely to depict the tawdriness of their contemporaries. The fact that so much historical fiction was written seems to show not only a desire to escape from the present, but an even greater desire to recall the courage and the spiritual resistance of the past. Sholem Asch, for example, wrote a number of novelettes and short stories that, though placed in a past era, portrayed a type of self-dedication still not uncommon among the Jews of eastern Europe. Joseph Opatoshu (1887-1956) was another teller of heroic historical tales. Meticulous in his research, he loved to show the Jew of old in the very center of the total civilization about him, whether in Roman Judea, or medieval Germany, or nineteenth century Poland.

Thus the surviving Yiddish literature between the two world wars, though completely westernized in style, form, and psychological approach, was a life-giving element for the Jews because of its ability to lay bare the positive and the negative forces that strove for mastery within the people. Hebrew literature of the same period underwent similar changes, but found its goal in being the literature of a nation in the making. It quickly lost its note of pessimism, for it could contrast the destruction of the old centers of Jewish life with the progress and hopefulness of the new community in Palestine. From a limited diaspora literature, read for parochial purposes, Hebrew writing turned national in the accepted sense of the term, that is, it covered every aspect of life, physical and spiritual, from the viewpoints of unity, of influence, and of strength. Bialik and Tchernichovsky, who had presaged this turn, were still the great masters, and even they acquired new enthusiasm as the community developed. The creation of a national literature within a single generation offers further evidence of Jewish vitality.

The rapidity of this development did not keep Hebrew literature from responding with sensitivity to the literary movements of the western world and of the environments in which the various authors grew up. Thus A. D. Gordon (1856-1922), the "prophet of labor," showed the unmistakable influence of Tolstoy; and at the same time, the more western ideas of man as the master of his fate and as the creator of a socialist community in which justice reigns supreme were also evident in his writing and teaching. Russian mysticism and western rationalism, economic determinism and Hebrew prophetism made up this strange personality guiding the beginnings of the Palestinian Hebrew settlement. Joseph Chaim Brenner (1881-1921), to cite another example from the earlier years of the century, also showed the effects of his Russian upbringing. It is not an accident that he translated Dostoevsky's *Crime and Punishment* into Hebrew. The sense of oppression and the prophetic seriousness that characterize his writing show him to have been a member of the generation that rebelled against Jewish aimlessness. He, like A. D. Gordon, was caught up in the Zionist movement, and as it did for Gordon, the Zionist movement gave goal to his yearnings, cohesiveness to his writing, and a surge of optimism to his work for the Jewish people. Zionism soon took such hold of the spirits of the Hebrew writers of that entire generation that one of their most gifted contemporaries, David Frishman (1860-1922), a thorough humanist, universalist, and good European, expressed his fears lest the humanism of Jewish tradition be eclipsed by theology on the one hand and nationalism on the other.

He need not have been afraid that any such development would take place, certainly not as long as the overwhelming majority of Hebrew writers came from an east European Jewish background colored by west European cosmopolitanism. Whether, like Avigdor Hameiri, they brought with them such strong recollections of the diaspora that their best writing had to be done on that background, or like A. A. Kabak, their forte was historical fiction, or like Samuel Joseph Agnon, they felt closest to the pietistic, Hasidic, mystical exaltation of the Jewish soul in the diaspora—they were all, novelists and poets alike, building a bridge, not only between the diaspora and the new community in the homeland, but also between the cultural experience of Europe and the new culture that was in process of creation. There were those, moreover, who were introducing still another ingredient into the nascent culture: men like Judah Burla and Chaim Hazaz, who undertook to build a cultural bridge between the new community and the oriental, Yemenite Jews with their entirely different traditions. But it is worth noting that whatever the cultural climate in which they grew up or which they tried to transfer to the old-new homeland, these descendants of the talmudists, halakhists, mystics, and Hasidim represent a literary tradition quite different from that of their Jewish predecessors of a generation or two ago. A European literary tradition prevails. Newer critics might have reversed David Frishman's fears and asked whether the humanism inherent in Jewish tradition, re-enforced by European literary influences, might eclipse the Jewish religious values one has a right to expect from a restored national life. The next few decades began to give a partial answer to this question.

The growth of the Hebrew literary movement in Europe and then in Palestine naturally affected the Jews of the United States. The men who stimulated Hebraic activity in the United States around the time of World War I and for decades thereafter were exclusively immigrants from eastern Europe or men who came from Palestine to occupy academic posts in various institutions of learning. Apart from their influence on Jewish education, they kept Hebrew literary activity alive by means of books and journals. Productivity was, to be sure, limited by the small number of readers; it was nevertheless one of the most extraordinary manifestations of the hold that Hebrew culture had on Jewish life that any progress at all was possible in the leveling American environment. This was largely the result of the efforts of a number of devoted men. Menahem Ribalow (1899-1954), for example, founded the journal *Hadoar* and kept it going for some thirty years by dint of great literary ability and organizational skill. Among the outstanding novelists, poets, and essayists whose labors continued into the sixth decade of the century were I. D. Berkowitz, who left to settle in Palestine in the 1920's, Hillel Bavli, Samuel L. Blank, Israel Efros, Harry Sackler, Eisig Silberschlag. There were signs that American subjects and attitudes might before long find expression in the Hebrew language. On the whole, however, the Hebrew literary movement in the diaspora has been so overshadowed by the literature of the homeland community as to seem but an echo of it.

2. THE AMERICAN SCENE

The number of Jews contributing to general American literature increased considerably during the twentieth century. The Jewish origin of these authors was far less conspicuous than it was in the case of the Jews writing in the German language; nor were the two groups comparable in literary standing, at least not until after World War II. Fannie Hurst, Edna Ferber, Maxwell Bodenheim, Ben Hecht—to mention a few of those better known as of Jewish origin— could tell a good story or write a good poem; they frequently showed great sensitivity to human values. But they could hardly be placed in the first literary rank. They knew how to reflect the turbulence of America's era of strife and progress, the country's social and cultural growing pains. Yet most of these men and women who participated in the development of American literature either were not interested in the herculean efforts that the Jewish immigrants were making to establish themselves in the New World or did not sense the drama of the immigrants' adjustment to American life.

Theodor Herzl (1860-1904). *(Zionist Archives and Library.)*

A New York sweatshop around the turn of the century.
(George Eastman House, Inc. Photo by Lewis Hine.)

A Lower East Side scene early in the century. *(Culver Service.)*

Shalom Aleichem (1859-1916).
(Yivo Institute.)

Chaim Nachman Bialik (1873-1934)
(Yivo Institute.)

Israel Zangwill (1864-1926).
(Zionist Archives and Library.)

Lillian D. Wald (1867-1940).
(Henry Street Settlement.)

Lee K. Frankel (1867-1931).
(American Jewish Archives.)

Tel Aviv in 1909. *(Zionist Archives and Library.)*

The first meeting, on November 27, 1914, of the Joint Distribution Committee for the Relief of Jewish War Sufferers. Among those taking part were (seated, left to right): Felix M. Warburg (chairman), Aaron Teitelbaum, Albert Lucas, Mrs. F. Friedman, Boris D. Bogen, Leon Sanders, Harry Fischel, Sholem Asch, Alexander Kahn, Jacob Milch, Harriet E. Lowenstein, Colonel Moses Schoenberg, M. Z. Margolies, Israel Friedlander, Paul Baerwald, Julius Levy, Peter Wiernik, Meyer Gillis, Harry Cutler, Cyrus Adler, Arthur Lehman, Jacob H. Schiff. *(American Jewish Joint Distribution Committee.)*

Jewish Legion recruits in Palestine, 1917. (*Zionist Archives and Library.*)

Foreign Office,

November 2nd, 1917.

Dear Lord Rothschild,

I have much pleasure in conveying to you, on behalf of His Majesty's Government, the following declaration of sympathy with Jewish Zionist aspirations which has been submitted to, and approved by, the Cabinet.

His Majesty's Government view with favour the establishment in Palestine of a national home for the Jewish people, and will use their best endeavours to facilitate the achievement of this object, it being clearly understood that nothing shall be done which may prejudice the civil and religious rights of existing non-Jewish communities in Palestine, or the rights and political status enjoyed by Jews in any other country"

I should be grateful if you would bring this declaration to the knowledge of the Zionist Federation.

Y. ing

Arthur James Balfour

The Balfour Declaration. *(Zionist Archives and Library.)*

Dr. Chaim Weizmann (1874-1952) and Dr. Stephen S. Wise (1874-1949).
(Zionist Archives and Library.)

Captured defenders of the Warsaw Ghetto. The German caption reads: "These bandits defended themselves with weapons." *(Zionist Archives and Library.)*

Jewish women in Auschwitz immediately after the
liberation in 1945. *(Yivo Institute.)*

Israel's Declaration of Independence, 1948. (*Israel Office of Information.*)

The inauguration of Chaim Weizmann as Israel's first President,
February 10, 1949. *(Israel Office of Information.)*

Members of Israel's Women's Army marching in Jerusalem on the tenth anniversary of the country's independence. *(Israel Office of Information.)*

The market of Mea Shearim quarter, Jerusalem, 1959.
(Israel Office of Information.)

Administration Building, Hebrew University, Jerusalem.
(Israel Office of Information.)

Aerial view of the settlement of Nahalal, Israel. *(Israel Office of Information.)*

This latter aspect of the American story fired the imagination of quite another group. Abraham Cahan's *The Rise of David Levinsky* (1917) may well be considered the first novel in English to set forth the spiritual tragedy that sometimes accompanied adjustment to the American environment. The next important contributor to what might be called the Jewish literature of adjustment was Ludwig Lewisohn (1882-1956). Lewisohn initially saw the situation in terms of thwarted ambition—the American Jew's burning desire to participate in the growth of America hurling itself vainly against the suspicions and prejudices of his non-Jewish neighbors—later he began to see that greater than the tragedy of Christian prejudice was the tragedy of the American Jew turning away from his own heritage.

The 1930's, perhaps in response to mounting anti-Semitism in American society, witnessed the emergence of several currents in a veritable stream of novels about the Jews. One group of Jewish authors saw immigrant Jewish life, in the midst of which they had grown up, in all its inward tenderness and spirituality, sometimes despite external ugliness. Such a view is expressed, for example, in Irving Fineman's *Hear, Ye Sons* (1933) and Henry Roth's *Call It Sleep* (1934). Nevertheless, even authors such as these gave vent occasionally to a note of irritation, something like a plaint against fate for tying them to a minority group weighted down, so to speak, by a strange and intellectually unaccepted heritage. The social hurt of the thirties clearly went deep.

Another, different group of Jewish authors saw only the ugliness, the strife, and the meanness inseparable from the struggles, burdens, and strangeness with which the immigrant and his immediate descendants had to cope. Michael Gold's *Jews Without Money* (1930), Jerome Weidman's *I Can Get It for You Wholesale* (1937), and Budd Schulberg's *What Makes Sammy Run?* (1940) are examples of the work of these writers. After reading these novels one might have supposed that the Jews acquiesced in all that the expanding anti-Semitic movement was then saying and in what Hitler had made popular among the masses. Another sort of novel was even worse, namely, the escape novel, in which self-hating authors described self-hating heroes seeking flight from hated Jewish fellowship, usually by way of intermarriage.

The story of the various literary movements among the Jews of the first four decades of the twentieth century offers a vivid reflection of the revolution that had taken place in the Jewish intellect and spirit. It appears that nothing was less true than the assumption that the Jew, emancipated in western Europe and in flight from eastern Europe, continued to stand aloof from western culture, that he insisted, so to speak, on carrying his ghetto with him. Quite the contrary: the Jews of every part of the world attempted, in their Jewish languages and in many others, to interpret the civilizations in the midst of which they lived and to join in the further development of these civilizations. In Yiddish and in Hebrew the results of the coalescence of the Jewish and the western spirit was productive of good, even significant, literature. The efforts of Jews to do what they could for the development of general culture were frequently at least as successful. But in such instances, whether the culture was expressed in German or in English, it usually overwhelmed the Jewish personality of the participant; all too often it obliterated it. In any case, it became clear in the fourth decade of the century that co-operation by Jews in the development of general culture was being scorned. This rejection turned out to be but an aspect of a deep malady; it represented a cleavage within the western spirit, and it foreshadowed the world-wide tragedy that soon followed.

3. RACIALISM IN AMERICA

One wonders about the inability of western civilization to meet its challenges during the period between the two world wars. It had apparently learned nothing from its experiences during four years of slaughter: "the war to end war" turned out to have been a war that engendered hate. The world continued to progress phenomenally in science, in the arts, and in industry; yet it seemed incapable of taming its fears and curbing its lust for battle. So the western world moved from crisis to crisis until it drifted into a second world war more terrible than the first. The maladies of our civilization became evident during the few decades that preceded World War II in a type of nationalism that in addition to its old faults, now became twisted into racialism, and in a set of religious and psychological values that while urging personal salvation and security, permitted conscience to atrophy. As usual, the failures of civilization in general became most obvious in the world's relation to its Jews.

Signs of the racialist direction in which nationalism was tending had been evident since the latter part of the nineteenth century. The apologies for colonialism on the bombastic grounds of "the white man's burden," the pseudo-scientific underpinnings of anti-Semitism, and the equally hypocritical concern about the purity of a "noble race," stemmed from the same source. Such ideas began to be expressed among the self-appointed upper class of American society and to seep down into the lower economic strata. Their diffusion in the United States was slow, because for one thing, about a third of the population was still conscious of its immigrant origins, and for another, industrial leaders were still convinced that they needed further recruits for their labor forces. The pompous proponents of Anglo-Saxon superiority at first remained merely prophets of doom. Soon after World War I, however, changed economic conditions deprived the labor argument of its potency. Besides, the newer generation had found a way of shedding its sense of immigrant inferiority by broadening the definition of the desirable racial strain. Instead of being limited to the Anglo-Saxon, it was extended to the "Nordic." This term included a much larger group—indeed, all white Protestants—and excluded the so-called Latins, the Slavs, and of course, the

Jews. A few decades later, when the Irish had become a political and economic force to be reckoned with, the religious qualification could be softened and Catholics too could be drawn into the magic circle. The "scientific" nature of this racial theory had been made plain in the work of Madison Grant, its chief American apostle. It was this aristocrat and arch-anti-Semite who made the fateful transition from the glorification of the Anglo-Saxon race to the enthronement of the Nordic. Such thinking, which became characteristic of many leaders of American opinion, contaminated American society.

Whether originally an importation from Europe, or a result of resentment on the part of older American families at being economically eclipsed and socially elbowed aside by newcomers, racialism, or nativism, was given a tremendous impetus by postwar conditions. The fever-pitch of wartime subsided as a result of the peace; anti-German and then anti-Bolshevist hysteria had to be replaced by another emotional outlet; the transition from a wartime to a peacetime economy involved a depression and was accompanied by labor troubles, which were blamed on foreigners. All this showed itself in the phenomenal development, during the 1920's, of the ridiculous and rowdy Ku Klux Klan and in a surprisingly widespread and ugly antiforeignism.

What Henry Adams, Madison Grant, and Lothrop Stoddard accomplished for the intellectuals, Henry Ford did for the masses. A simple-minded man, he like tens of millions of others sought a simple explanation of all the ills of the world. Nothing seemed simpler than a plot by a people whose survival and presumed prosperity had always appeared inexplicable except on the assumption of God's special blessing or of devilish, sinister plotting. Ford fell victim to the persuasiveness of a former propagandist for czarist Russia, who elaborated on a plot of the Jews, first to ruin, then to seize control of the world. "The Protocols of the Elders of Zion" were the supposed minutes of secret meetings of Jewish leaders towards the end of the nineteenth century (a time that coincided with that of the first World Zionist Congress). Though an obvious hoax, based as was later disclosed, upon an old satire directed against Napoleon III, the Protocols were given wide currency by Ford's *Dearborn Independent* and were accepted as true by every frightened nativist in the country. An atmosphere was created that helped deepen prejudice, even among those who recognized the story's stupidity.

Under such influences, the United States during the 1920's became for many Jews and members of other minorities a land of restrictions rather than opportunities. With the descendants of many former immigrant groups charged with "mongrelizing" the "pure Nordic blood," with citizens of foreign origin under suspicion of fomenting labor and social unrest, with prospective immigrants from eastern and southern Europe held up as inferior, One-Hundred-Per-Cent Americanism came to mean first of all the restriction of immigration. A literacy test, finally passed over President Wilson's veto in 1917, proved completely ineffective in meeting the situation when large-scale immigration resumed in 1920. Each month over 50,000 immigrants crowded Ellis Island; among them were a large number of Jews and a great many Italians and Slavs. This influx frightened the nativists out of their wits. The law of 1921 limited immigration to five per cent of the total foreign-born population of the United States according to the census of 1910, and it was provided that the total number of immigrants, during any one year, should not exceed a quarter of a million. Still the restrictionists were not satisfied. In 1924 a new law was passed in which the basic census was that of 1890 and each nationality was limited to two per cent of the number it had had in the population at that time. Although families of citizens were exempted from this calculation, immigration was in fact severely limited, except for the so-called Nordic countries, most of which could never fill the quotas allotted them. The United States thus legally adopted a racialist policy; Italians, Slavs, Greeks, and indirectly, also Jews were, in effect, declared inferior and unwanted. Prejudice, under the guise of science, had won a resounding victory, one that could not be undone even when, a few years later, prosperity having returned and hysteria having abated, the saner and more truly American elements again prevailed.

The spirit of restriction extended as well to other areas of life. It not only kept more Jews from coming into the country, but also limited the activities and opportunities of those already in the United States. Divisive practices were shameless. Hotels, resorts, and dwellings, as well as jobs, were closed to Jews and to some other minorities. At the same time, Christian restrictionism and exclusiveness were justified by the assertion that Jews were clannish. Most shocking was the complete surrender to the prevalent prejudices by leaders of American culture. Quota systems had long existed in the more important professional schools; now similar quotas were adopted by undergraduate colleges, even those functioning in large centers of population. Culture, like banking and automobile manufacturing, was going nativist. Much of the literature of the day reflected this spirit.

4. THE FLOWERING OF THE DEFENSE ORGANIZATIONS

The Jews of the United States were thus faced with a new situation—not new in Jewish history, for it recalled, not too vaguely, conditions and attitudes that had led, in centuries gone by, to their exclusion from Christian and Moslem society—but new in the United States. Previous instances of discrimination had been few and scattered; now, with the number of Jews in the country greatly increased, such instances became widespread and assumed the aspects of social policy. The situation was all the more painful because the American Jew had fallen in love with America and took pride in its freedoms and its spirit of equality. He drew solace from the knowledge that many true liberals were raising their voices to criticize the prevalent hatreds, and he put his hopes in the fundamentals of Americanism. Nevertheless, he felt that some action on his part was called for. To be sure, for the time being, nothing could be done about the restrictions on immigration. The harshness of the law, as distinct from the spirit behind it, had been somewhat mitigated by the exemption from its operation of close relatives of American citizens. Besides, Latin America, South Africa, and parts of western Europe were still available as places of refuge for the hard-pressed of eastern Europe. But something had to be done about the invasions of the personal rights of the Jewish people and about the wild accusations that were being leveled against them.

Although the Jews of the country had not achieved unity, they did occasionally succeed in speaking with one voice. Thus, in December 1920, twenty of the most important nation-wide Jewish organizations responded to a call by the American Jewish Committee and jointly issued a repudiation of the charges identifying Jews with Bolshevism and with the Protocols. Again, in 1924, when about 15,000 would-be Jewish immigrants, on their way to the United States under the law of 1921, were stranded at ports of embarkation because they were unable to comply with the requirements of the new law of 1924, there was wholehearted co-operation in dealing with this problem. The American Jewish Committee and the American Jewish Congress convoked a national conference and created the Emergency Committee for Jewish Refugees, which in the course of a few years, helped these emigrants to return to their former countries or to find homes elsewhere.

On the whole, however, Jewish defense efforts varied in accordance with the nature of the groups and classes into which American Jewry was divided or the leadership these groups and classes followed. The American Jewish Committee, though less exclusive than formerly, was still representative of the wealthier and older stratum, and pursued the quiet, dignified methods it had adopted from its inception. In letters to individuals and in public statements, Louis Marshall, the Committee's president, denounced and refuted anti-Jewish assertions and publications. He scored his great-est success when, in 1927, he obtained from Henry Ford a complete retraction of, and apology for, the libels and insin-uations his publications had been spreading for almost a decade.

Another defense organization, the Anti-Defamation League, was an arm of the B'nai B'rith, which had just entered upon a period of rapid expansion as a result, in part, of having opened its membership to growing numbers of second-generation east European Jews. The ADL, organ-ized in 1913, was therefore in a sense representative of the middle-class Jew eager for a more direct and vocal defense of his rights and his good name. It undertook to answer all attacks, to explain all presumed shortcomings, to refute every accusation. The results of this task proved to be some-what disappointing. Very few of the masses of non-Jews, who were easily led to suspect the Jews when some fiery dema-gogue described them as satanic conspirators, ever got to read or came to hear the defense. In fact, the demagogues used the ADL's efforts to unmask their dishonesty as evi-dence of persecution at the hands of the Jews. On the other hand, vocal defense also had considerable advantages. The non-Jews, whether infected with anti-Semitism or not, got to know that the Jews were reacting vigorously to the accu-sations fired in their direction. Fighting back brought a measure of respect.

The American Jewish Congress, originally formed only for the purpose of representing American Jewry at the Ver-sailles Peace Conference in 1919, was followed by a perma-nent organization established in 1922. It made an effort to be representative of the entire American Jewish community by inviting to membership both national organizations and specially established local groups. Its program was broad, including civic and national, defensive and educational ac-tivities. It recognized that a minority's firmest allies were the liberal forces of the Nation, that all minorities, whether racial or religious, faced common problems and must come to one another's defense, and that the American tradition of democracy was the best guarantee of personal and religious security. On the assumption that no apologies were needed for a minority's right to exist, the Congress from the first tried to put the anti-Semites and the reactionaries on the defensive. This broad, liberal, fighting program fitted the character of Dr. Stephen S. Wise perfectly, and it became characteristic of the Congress of which he was the head from its establishment until his death. The Congress, not limiting its activities to defense, participated actively in Zionist work and early adopted a program of adult Jewish education. Democracy and good sense demanded that if an organization expected the intelligent participation of its members, it must make them aware of the background and the nature of its activities.

Here then were three different responses to the problem of anti-Semitism in a democracy. The differences noted have been, of course, variations of emphasis rather than delimitations of policy. There was considerable overlapping of activity among all of the defense organizations. It may well be that they arrested the spread of the moral ailment of anti-Semitism during the later 1920's. The next decade, however, brought new and even greater danger. Until the 1920's, anti-Semitic activities in the United States and elsewhere in the west were un-co-ordinated. Now, a determined enemy of the Jews, one well supplied with vast resources, took control; the situation became ominous on a worldwide scale.

5. THE COMMUNIST AND FASCIST ATTACKS

The 1920's witnessed the beginnings in Europe of the trend toward the tragedy that was to overwhelm the world and destroy more than a third of the Jewish people. The framers of the Treaty of Versailles had thought to safeguard the peace by imposing a democratic system of government upon the states defeated in the war and upon those that emerged from the breakup of the Russian and Austrian empires.

They had hoped to assure the reign of justice among peoples by creating a League of Nations and by including in the League's charter those clauses for the protection of minorities which the representatives of the Jews had urged upon them. Unfortunately, democracy was alien to most of the nations in central and eastern Europe, while international justice proved to be an ideal for which the nations of the world were not yet prepared.

The mild, socialistically-inclined republic established in Germany was spiritually not strong enough to combat the resentment against defeat that gnawed at the hearts of the population. The assassination of Walter Rathenau (1922), a very able leader of the new government who had been working toward a lasting peace with France, was the first open expression of bitterness which took an anti-Jewish turn. No matter how stupid it sounds, it is a fact that the reactionaries and ultranationalists of Germany accepted the theory that the defeat was due to Germany's betrayal by its Jews. The majority of the population at first ridiculed the small National Socialist group led by the ex-corporal Hitler; but nothing was done to counteract his insidious antigovernment propaganda, which used anti-Semitism as its means for attracting party members. It appeared silly for a government to imagine that its survival depended on the defense of the Jews; yet that proved to be the case. As for the German Jews themselves, staunch German patriots, thoroughly assimilated into German culture, they could not imagine that their Christian compatriots would let them down by succumbing to Hitler's rabid doctrines. They did what they could to present facts in self-defense. The rest of the National Socialist program seemed to them understandable enough, for many German Jews shared the widespread resentment against the Treaty of Versailles. Like most Germans, they did not think that Hitler would ever attain power: a civilized people like the Germans, they thought, could never succumb to the rowdy tactics of the Nazis. And they were certain that if, by some remote chance, he did win an election, he would never carry his anti-Jewish threats into execution.

In the 1920's the problems connected with the Jews of eastern Europe seemed much more serious than those of the German Jews. There was, first of all, the question of Jews in Russia. The Bolshevist government had established itself firmly and embarked ruthlessly upon communizing the country. This meant a complete transformation of Jewish life. From being largely middlemen, Jews had to turn to artisanship. The younger people could perhaps adjust themselves, but the middle-aged and the older people could find no place in farming or industry. They were reduced to performing the most menial tasks, or failing that, to starvation. For a few brief years in the middle 1920's, Lenin felt compelled to slow the pace of Russian communization, and his New Economic Policy temporarily eased the situation of the mercantile class of which Jews formed a large part. During the respite some adjustments could be made; but there is every reason to believe that the ultimate solution of the problem of the Jewish middle-aged came through death rather than adjustment. An even more serious problem confronted Judaism as a religion. Officially, anti-Semitism was banned; though, as subsequent events proved, the facts differed from the law. But anti-Judaism was given free rein, with the communists of Jewish origin carrying this program through with incredible ferocity. Most synagogues, like many churches, were closed or confiscated. Jewish religious education was forbidden by law. The teaching of Hebrew and adherence to Zionism were declared counter-revolutionary. Observance of Jewish law and tradition put a person under suspicion and was likely to deprive him of his means of livelihood. Thus not only was the survival of the three million Russian Jews jeopardized, but the survival of Judaism itself was also imperiled.

On the other hand, Jews were recognized as a nationality. Yiddish was declared one of the official languages in addition to Russian. The Jews of the larger cities could, if they so desired, send their children to schools in which Yiddish was the language of instruction. Literary and scholarly activity in Yiddish was permitted and actually developed, and a Yiddish counterpart of the official newspaper *Pravda* bore the name *Emmes,* in the Yiddish, not the Hebrew, spelling of the word. Moreover, whether to gain the sympathy of western Jews, or to cast doubts upon reports of the cruel fate to which the process of communization had subjected the Russian Jews, or to lessen the appeal that the promise of Palestine was having for some of these Jews, the Soviet government promised to establish in southern Russia a Jewish agricultural settlement that might some day become an autonomous district within the state. The already-established population of the territory chosen for this settlement evidently offered strenuous objections to the plan, hostility to Jews apparently not being quite dead. When the initial plan for a Jewish settlement could not be put into effect, the prospect was transferred to the dreary wastelands of Siberia. The outlook for distant Biro-Bidjan as a future Jewish state was portrayed in glowing colors. Twenty years later, the district still had no more than a few thousand Jewish inhabitants.

The most hopeful part of the world's Jewish population in the 1920's, and the most spiritually promising, was still concentrated in the new and revived states east of Germany: Poland, Latvia, Lithuania, and Czechoslovakia. Under the Minority Treaties new prospects for Jewish physical and spiritual development opened up in these countries. The only one that had protested strenuously and indignantly against being compelled to put its minorities under international protection had been Poland, the very one that had both the largest number of Jews and the worst record of persecution in the immediate, as well as the more distant past. The only one where the Jews were not especially concerned whether or not they enjoyed the rights guaranteed under the Minority Treaties was Czechoslovakia, whose record with respect to such rights had been good, and whose leaders, Thomas G. Masaryk and Eduard Beneš, could be trusted to safeguard democracy. To a greater or lesser extent, therefore, the Jews of Poland and Czechoslovakia and of the other states, which had promised to abide by the minorities system, organized themselves into communities with power to regulate their internal Jewish life without governmental interference. They could, if they desired, establish a school system and receive support for it from state taxes. At the same time, they enjoyed every right of citizenship in their respective countries. Feeling relatively secure, the Jews, with help from the American Joint Distribution Committee, began to rebuild Jewish life. There was, of course, no unanimity among the Jews in any of these countries; the arguments among the Hebraists, secularists, and religionists of every shade were sometimes acrimonious, and each group insisted on a school system of its own. Nonetheless, it seemed obvious that Jewish life had a future.

Unfortunately, the minorities system soon began to be sabotaged by the governments concerned. Born out of racial consciousness, each of the Slavic states pursued a racialist policy. To advance the interests of the dominant race, the governments discriminated in its favor in the vast civil service networks and in the industrial and commercial activities directly or indirectly under governmental control. Co-operatives established by these governments competed with Jewish merchants, but employed no Jews. Before the end of the 1920's the amount of state subsidy to which the Jews were entitled began to shrink and Jewish representatives in government departments were being eliminated. The Poles, of course, set the pace for this policy; Latvia and Lithuania followed close behind. The Jews were intimidated into not calling their fatherlands to account before the League of Nations, while of itself the League, that is, the combination of great powers, was morally too weak to act. By the 1930's the Slavic nations received support and encouragement in their anti-Jewish policies from the more terrible example of Nazi Germany. Thus another achievement of the peace following World War I presaged, by its failure, the greater tragedy into which mankind was to be plunged.

6. AN EMPIRE AND ITS CONSCIENCE

The 1920's proved disappointing also in the progress towards the realization of the glowing promise of a Jewish Palestine. Again the constructive work founded on faith, hope, and idealism was done by the Jews, while the non-Jews—Christians and Moslems alike—either attempted to block every Jewish step forward or refrained from giving their promised help.

The decade opened with the Third Aliyah in full swing. From 1919 to 1923 some 35,000 *halutzim* (pioneers) immigrated. They built roads and drained swamps; they established colonies and brought new land under cultivation. They made the Valley of Jezreel blossom as in days of old, and they made cooperative labor a reality. Never before had the world seen such peasants, so avid for culture, so deeply interested in ideas, so consciously a part of the world's hopes. Their successors, from 1924 to 1930, who constituted the so-called Fourth Aliyah, were of a somewhat different type. Also east European Jews, mostly Polish, their immigration into Palestine was motivated by despair over conditions in Poland, by the closing of the gates in America, and above all, by the promise of a national Jewish community in Palestine. They were rather older than those who had constituted the Third Aliyah and therefore comparatively few of them became farmers; the majority gravitated to the cities. They raised the population of Tel Aviv from about 14,000 in the early 1920's to close to 40,000 at the end of the decade, and they developed other towns as well. Their interests tended toward commerce and industry, which they developed despite the temporary economic setback the country suffered in 1926 and 1927. Thus Palestine acquired, in the decade following the granting of the mandate to Britain, an active and productive population that rose from

56,000 at the end of World War I, to 84,000 by 1922, and to 175,000 by the end of the twenties.

Britain had been appointed by the League of Nations as a partner of the Jews in the creation of a Jewish homeland in Palestine. While it performed well the administrative tasks of government, it failed completely to implement the primary aspect of the partnership. Instead, it saw its duty to the Empire first, that is, it kept a careful watch lest Jewish interests advance too far and too quickly against the presumed interests of the Arabs. No doubt the British were impressed by awakening Arab nationalism, and desiring to strengthen Britain's position in the Middle East, sought to show themselves as the Arab's friends. In general, this was the era of appeasement; the world was destined to take a long time to discover that appeasement only whets the appetite of the appeased. Bit by bit, the interpretation of the Balfour Declaration was whittled down. The painful steps in this process cannot be detailed here. It took the form of administrative orders and investigating commissions and White Papers; of granting public lands to the Arabs while the Jews had to purchase land at fantastic prices; of curtailment of Jewish immigration on specious principles; of loudly voiced sympathy for the poor *fellahin* (Arab peasants)—who in reality had never before "had it so good" —and irritation with the Jews. Here, in brief, was a series of government actions that not only negated the promise of a Palestinian homeland, but also made it impossible for Jew and Arab to get together, and by favoring the Arab side in the dispute, encouraged the latter to riot and bloodshed.

The mandate provided that a "Jewish Agency," representative of all the Jews of the world who were interested in the project, should help bring the homeland into being. There was need for the active co-operation of a great many prominent, well-to-do, and influential Jews, some of whom were, in fact, outspoken non-Zionists. The task of building the homeland needed not only their means but also the prestige they enjoyed among the peoples of the world. It needed, above all, a united Jewish front in the face of the growing coolness of the British Colonial Office to the Jewish aspect of the mandate. But it took some years of planning and negotiation for the various groups of non-Zionists to agree among themselves, and for all of them together to come to terms with the Zionists. This result was finally achieved in the summer of 1929 after patient planning by Dr. Chaim Weizmann, president of the World Zionist Organization. At Zurich, Switzerland, a group consisting of some of the most distinguished Jews of the world, non-Zionists as well as Zionists, adopted a set of regulations for the Jewish Agency called for in the mandate. In helping to achieve this goal, the great American Jew, Louis Marshall, who died a few days later, rendered the last of his many services to his people.

But even while Jews were congratulating themselves on this achievement, news arrived of another and more serious anti-Jewish outbreak in Palestine. More than a hundred Jews were killed, almost two hundred were wounded, and several isolated colonies were destroyed. The two events, occurring simultaneously, symbolized the decade's ceaseless organizational and constructive efforts on the part of the Jews in the face of the lack of government co-operation, intrigue, violence, and destruction. In the next decade, the forces of destruction were to gain complete and unchallenged dominance.

7. THE RISE AND SPREAD OF FASCISM

The fourth decade of the twentieth century actually opened in the latter half of 1929 with the misfortune of an economic depression, one that grew in severity during the next few years. Widespread unemployment turned dissatisfaction into bitter discontent, and discontent simmered into rebelliousness. Two revolutionary authoritarian movements profited from the situation: Russian communism and that travesty on the social state which had been named fascism by Mussolini, the Italian mountebank dictator. Adolf Hitler's National Socialist Democratic Labor Party improved on this, combining its vague socialism with virulent racialism, aggressive nationalism, and murderous anti-Semitism. As the decade progressed, militarism, fascism, Nazism, and communism gained control of a large part of the world; while, trying to maintain peace, the rest groped helplessly in the midst of economic and social upheavals to avoid the infection of these flagrant denials of civilization. As a result of its weakness and vacillation, the democratic west saw China and Ethiopia conquered by force of arms; Finland and Czechoslovakia reduced to servitude; Russia, Germany, and Spain subjected to bloody purges; and its own freedom and human dignity openly disparaged and undermined from within. The League of Nations, weak at the start, proved utterly helpless, and almost every other hopeful result of World War I was practically nullified. Under these circumstances, it was inevitable that the Jews should become the greatest sufferers in Europe.

Events in eastern Europe, in Palestine, and in some western countries had been disturbing enough; but all such evil trends and conditions were dwarfed for the rest of the decade by the horrors that centered in Germany. It seemed incredible that Germany would succumb to such barbarism, that its scientists would yield their almost tedious adherence to facts, its clergy yield conscience, and its cultured element yield common sense. Yet that is what happened in 1933, and the first plank of the Nazi program that Hitler implemented when he rose to power was that threatening the civil, political, and economic status of the Jews.

After the first outburst of physical attacks on the Jews was over, Nazism having been given a chance to express its gutter nature, Hitler let loose a number of anti-Jewish decrees aimed at removing Jewish influence from German society. Jews were summarily dismissed from civil and academic posts. They could not act as lawyers for non-Jewish clients. Unofficially, but quite effectively, a boycott was enforced against business owned or managed by Jews. Booted and armed young Nazis, frequently sons or hirelings of competitors, turned customers away from stores. Objectors, and those on a previously prepared list of Jewish leaders and other opponents of Nazism, were arrested, beaten, and sent off to that typically Nazi institution, the concentration camp.

In view of what was to happen later, all this chicanery and brutality seems fairly mild. Hitler and his aides evidently still feared the reaction of the rest of the world. But only the Jews reacted, and not even all of them. The American Jewish Congress, under the leadership of Stephen S. Wise, organized vast protest meetings and urged all decent people to avoid buying German goods. Other Jews, however, advised caution, lest the Nazis become even more violent. Such advice was based on the expectation that the civilized world would bring pressure to bear on the new German government. But the so-called civilized world did nothing of the kind. Perhaps if it had, the entire chain of gruesome events of the next decade might have been avoided.

Within the next few years, every conceivable humiliation was visited upon the Jewish population of Germany. Before long, every means of livelihood was closed to the Jews. In 1934, in the infamous Nuremberg laws, they were officially deprived of German citizenship and the term "Jew" was defined by decree to mean anyone, regardless of his religion, who had one Jewish grandparent. Thus the needed target for hatred was broadened. It was further enlarged with the annexation of Austria in March 1938. On November 10, 1938, a day of open rioting was declared in revenge for the killing by a Jew of a minor German diplomatic official in Switzerland. That day, almost all the synagogues in Germany went up in flames.

Six hundred thousand men, women, and children, and as many more when those of Austria and Czechoslovakia were added, faced annihilation. Practically all of them were above the average in culture and among the foremost in commerce, science, and the arts. Who came to their aid? Unquestionably there were German Christians whose hearts bled for them and some who suffered exile or imprisonment because of their outspoken sympathy for the persecuted Jews. But these were a tiny number and made no impression whatever on the general population. Some churchmen spoke up. Pope Pius XI issued an encyclical on March 14, 1937, in which he opposed racism and condemned the attacks on the Jewish Bible. "Spiritually," the Pope said, "we are all Semites." Even before this, Cardinal Faulhaber of Munich and several other prelates had objected to the inclusion of converts to Christianity among those considered Jews. In 1938 the Archbishop of Canterbury and other members of the Church of England spoke up more directly against the persecution of the Jews, as did a number of Protestant clergymen in Europe outside of Germany; within Germany, however, the Protestant clergy remained, on the whole, silent. Such limited, indirect, and rather polite criticism of savagery rampant did not offer much evidence of a sensitive religious spirit in wide circles of western civilization.

With their advent to power, the Nazis embarked upon a world-wide anti-Semitic propaganda campaign. Every person of German ancestry anywhere in the world was a potential apologist for Nazism; every anti-Semite was a Nazi collaborator. An especially virulent campaign was conducted in the United States and was almost successful in persuading the population that to attempt interference with Nazi plans was to fall victim to a Jewish plot. So laden with racialism and anti-Semitism, or so callous, had the world's atmosphere become that little refuge could be found for the fugitives from Hitler's fury. Throughout the decade, the Jewish leaders of western countries went hat-in-hand to statesmen and parliamentary committees pleading for the admittance of even small numbers of the fugitives. It was not enough to point out that a refusal meant condemning thousands to death; one had to assure these representatives of civilized Christian nations that the prospective immigrants would not become public charges, or that they were young people of ability and skill, or that they were children who had to be saved from the tiger's paws. Within the United States, as in some other countries, the Jews added to their already burdensome philanthropies the National Refugee Service through which they kept the promise exacted from them that the new immigrants would not become a burden on the general community. In the end, Great Britain, between 1933 and 1939, admitted about 75,000; down to its entrance into the war, the United States admitted some 175,000. The international Evian Conference of 1938, called for the purpose of finding more places of refuge, ended in failure.

Soon after the Nazis captured Germany, the Jews of that country embarked on two constructive activities: they tried to send the very young Jewish children out of the country; and they established training centers for young people so that, equipped with some manual skill, they would be prepared to go to Palestine. Families and individuals, frequently Christians, in various countries like Britain, the Netherlands, and Denmark, adopted some of the children. Henrietta Szold, then a permanent resident of Palestine, organized a Youth Aliyah for the transportation of children to Palestine and for their upbringing there. The young people, along with those older ones who could do so, made their way to Palestine through ordinary channels, though a good many had to circumvent British limiting regulations and enter the country illegally. Altogether the Fifth Aliyah, which consisted mostly of German refugees, brought about 100,000 Jews into Palestine before the outbreak of World War II.

The Palestinian Arabs, however, decided to join in the widespread anti-Jewish barbarities by means of another uprising. Although the Jews responded with a policy of nonresistance (*havlagah*), five hundred Jews were killed between 1936 and 1939; thousands were wounded. If, on the one hand, nonresistance had no effect whatever in stopping the Arabs' war against the Jews, the danger from the Arabs did not, on the other hand, stop the Jews from continuing the development of the country with the aid of the energetic and capable newcomers. Britain, of course, sent another investigation commission; its report led to a further effort to appease the Arabs. The White Paper of 1939 limited the number of Jewish immigrants to 15,000 a year for the next five years. The policy was intended to make certain that the Jews would remain permanently a minority of the country's population.

The effect that such palpable hostility in almost every part of the world had on the Jews of the democratic countries was to intensify their defense efforts. A new defensive organization had come into existence in 1933 in the form of the Jewish Labor Committee. Because of its contacts with general labor organizations, this body was able to exert influence on the latter to resist Nazi anti-Jewish propaganda in their ranks. The American Jewish Committee, in touch with Jewish leaders everywhere, including Germany, was able to compile and analyze the propaganda of the Nazi agents in the United States, unmask them, and reveal their lies. In 1932 and again in 1934, the American Jewish Congress called meetings of representatives of various European communities for the purpose of taking joint action to combat mounting anti-Jewish feeling. In 1936 the World Jewish Congress came into being for the defense of Jewish rights, Stephen S. Wise and Nahum Goldmann being the leaders. The Congress promoted the anti-Nazi boycott, organized public protest meetings, and vigorously attacked every denial of human rights. The Anti-Defamation League of the B'nai B'rith concentrated on watching the activities of native fascists and rabble rousers. Before long, all the defense organizations joined in a General Jewish Council.

The type of danger they had to guard against was exemplified by the activities of the Reverend Dr. Charles E. Coughlin, a Roman Catholic priest in Detroit. In October 1938 he began a series of weekly anti-Jewish broadcasts over a national radio hookup. In addition to his spoken diatribes, he published direct and slyly indirect attacks on the Jews. A so-called Christian Front, formed in New York City under his sponsorship, carried on a violent anti-Jewish campaign through street meetings, the boycotting of Jewish merchants, and other means. The Jewish defense organizations attempted to answer him in public statements, and privately appealed to Coughlin's ecclesiastical superiors. He was eventually silenced, but with shocking reluctance and after surprising delay. Another source of anti-Jewish attacks was isolationism in the United States. Isolationist groups charged that, because of their hatred of Nazism, American Jews were stirring up public opinion in favor of intervention in what was a purely European war. The raucous isolationist voices were silenced only by the Japanese attack on Pearl Harbor on December 7, 1941.

V

· ·

The Ordeal of Civilization

· ·

·

1. THE TRIUMPH OF SAVAGERY

Since Hitler's war was prepared for, and entered upon, to establish German supremacy over the rest of mankind, it was natural that the Jews should be the first sufferers and that the murderous spirit of Nazism should be directed most ruthlessly against them. This is not the place to speak of the travail of all civilization, of the machine-gunning of fugitives, of the bombing of cities, of the oppression of populations. Eventually, the Nazis lost the war against their enemies east and west, but as has been repeatedly pointed out, they won the physical war against the Jews. Six million people died, many of them murdered in cold blood, only because their nature, tradition, and hopes were the antithesis of Nazism. Thousands of communities—among them, some antedated the presumed native communities of the lands of which they were part—all of which had made significant contributions to local and to European civilization, were wiped off the face of the earth. To say that the six years of World War II constituted the most disastrous period in Jewish history in almost two millennia is to presume too much on the power of words to transmit a sense of tragedy. Only a Jeremiah could describe it—the beastliness and the heroism. What made the situation the more horrible was that the conscience of the rest of the world was so little stirred both at that time and later.

There were, to be sure, almost entire nations, like the Danes and the Dutch, and many individuals among the British, Norwegians, and French who defied the Nazis and did their utmost to save their Jewish neighbors. Most of them acted out of sheer humanity. Some, especially French Catholics, in their zeal to "save" the children they had hidden, had them baptized, and in some of these cases, the protectors of the children refused, after the war, to restore them to their Jewish families.

People who, at great personal risk, came to the aid of the hunted, kept alive faith in the essential goodness of human nature. But there were others, far more numerous, in the invaded countries to the east who helped the Nazis in their destruction of the Jewish population. Poles, Rumanians, Hungarians, and Ukrainians by the thousands, fawning upon their conquerors, outdid them in brutality. In France there were few such traitors to humanity, but the Vichy government was dominated by the Nazis and paid them the tribute of imitation by disfranchising the Jews and interning them, along with Christian liberals and patriots, in concentration camps.

Unarmed and completely in their enemy's hands, the peaceful Jewish populations of the countries overrun by the Nazis were stunned by their fate. It was hard to believe that human beings could be so coldly brutal, so completely merciless as the invaders. A small number of young Jews here and there succeeded in eluding the Germans and organizing themselves into bands of guerrilla fighters. They had to contend not only against the Germans but often against another, almost equally bad, enemy, the Christian partisans. The vast majority of the Jews in eastern Europe, now herded into ghettos, at first refused to believe that their extermination had been decreed. The Nazis kept the torture chambers and the crematories secret. But eventually the secret leaked out. Then some sort of resistance, hopeless though it was bound to be, was organized. The smuggling of small arms to the ghettos took a long time; it had to be done piece by piece, and even so, arms were hard to come by because non-Jewish underground forces gave the Jews but grudging co-operation. In time, several ghettos revolted, the biggest and most spectacular revolt being that in Warsaw, which began on April 19, 1943, and continued for some days, until almost every Jewish fighter lay dead in the ruins.

Several countries in southeastern Europe, however, though under the heel of the Nazis during the first years of the war, did not remain completely under their control. An arrangement with the governments of Rumania and Hungary, each with about three quarters of a million Jews in 1941, was possible, and permission might have been obtained for the emigration of a considerable number of Jews. But where were they to go? No country engaged in the war against Germany was willing to permit them to enter—and to this extent these countries and their leaders must share in the guilt of the eventual murder of hundreds of thousands. There was room in Palestine. But Britain, ever hopeful of Arab co-operation, which it never got, refused to rescind or relax the immigration restrictions of the shameful White Paper of 1939. A few of those Jews who escaped from the European furnaces succeeded in making their surreptitious way across the Palestinian border, to the intense indignation of the British officials in Palestine.

The Arabs everywhere in the Middle East were, in fact, openly in sympathy with the Nazi cause. The propaganda of the ex-mufti, who had eluded the British and made common cause with the Nazis, bore fruit. An Iraqi rebellion had to be put down by military force. The Egyptians hailed with joy every advance made in North Africa by the German General Rommel. The Jews of Palestine, on the other hand, offered, early in the war, to organize a considerable force and join the British armies. The British government managed to put all sorts of obstacles in the way of any such plan, even to the absurdity of limiting the number of Jews in a Palestinian force to the very small number of Palestinian Arabs who volunteered. The British apparently preferred defeat to giving the Jews any ground for claims to postwar treatment worthy of allies. Not until 1944 were the Jews of Palestine permitted to organize a separate battalion. Despite all obstacles, considerable numbers of Palestine Jews participated, as groups within the British armies, in battles on almost every front. Behind the lines, in Palestine, Jews performed invaluable auxiliary service. An occasional word of commendation was given them by several regional British commanders; but officially the British government acted as though none of this had happened. The Jews were, as the saying went in those years, Britain's "anonymous allies."

When the fighting ended with the occupation of Germany, Allied soldiers freed the tortured and emaciated concentration camp inmates whom the Nazis had not destroyed in their final burst of fury. The furnaces and crematoriums in which so many human beings had perished were now uncovered. The feeling of revulsion that seized the soldiers was carried over to the civilian populations of the western nations. Now the world learned the truth about Nazism, which it had refused to believe when the Jews told it. In the course of the next few years, some—by no means many —of the perpetrators of the most outrageous cruelties were condemned to death or imprisonment, and for a while ex-Nazis were in disgrace. Within five years, however, the process was reversed: one after another the condemned and imprisoned perpetrators of inhuman horrors were released. This was done by communist as well as noncommunist governments. In rare instances, when the inhumanity of the released Nazi had been more than usually revolting, the German government itself, in response to protests, placed him on trial in a German court. Yet many former Nazis were admitted to government service and placed in positions of influence. That was the extent to which the world's conscience stirred over the fate of six million innocent victims.

2. THE REMNANTS OF A PEOPLE

Every aspect of Jewish life during the postwar decade (1945-1955) was affected by the consciousness of two things: the disappearance of Jewish communities in the European diaspora and the rise of the Jewish state in Palestine. The second was, to a very large extent, the creative response to the first, while both together evoked forces that have not ceased to modify the lives of the remaining diaspora communities.

At the century's opening, the Jewishly most promising communities were those of eastern and central Europe. Numerically, they accounted for more than half of the world's Jewish population. The ratio was decreased somewhat by the growth of the new diaspora communities in America and elsewhere; but as late as the outbreak of World War II, the older communities remained preponderant. The contrast between the last available statistics (1939 or 1940) before the war and the best available figures after its end is instructive. Both sets of figures are offered in round numbers for those countries that came under Nazi rule.

	Jewish Population in 1939 or 1940	Jewish Population in 1945 or 1946	Losses
Germany	150,000	20,000	130,000
Austria	190,000	4,000	186,000
Italy	45,000	35,000	10,000
Poland	3,250,000	45,000	3,205,000
Rumania	750,000	425,000	325,000
Hungary	725,000	143,000	582,000
Czechoslovakia	360,000	100,000	260,000
Bulgaria	48,000	28,000	20,000
Yugoslavia	75,000	15,000	60,000
Greece	75,000	10,000	65,000
France	250,000	130,000	120,000
The Netherlands	140,000	35,000	105,000
Belgium	75,000	20,000	55,000
Luxembourg	5,000	1,200	3,800
Denmark	2,500	1,500	1,000
Norway	1,300	700	600

In some instances, the reduction noted was due to emigration. In Germany itself, for example, about 360,000 of the half million Jews there in 1932 are said to have left by 1939. Most of those who remained anywhere in Europe were, of course, exterminated without being recorded in the figures noted above. Many thousands of Polish Jews fled into Russia before the Nazi invasion of the latter, though apparently not so many as was once supposed. In any case, there are no reliable figures for the situation in Russia in general. The Nazi invasion of Russia in 1941 and 1942 overran the very districts inhabited by many Jews, who were treated by the Nazis and their collaborators with the same barbarity as that meted out to Jews elsewhere. Certainly the Jewish losses in the Ukraine exceeded a million. It seems clear, therefore, that the six million figure as the number of Jews done to death during the war years is close to the truth. The number of Jews in the world was reduced by at least a third. The reduction in the spiritual potential is, of course, incalculable.

It is well to recall, moreover, that the termination of hostilities did not bring to an end the tragedy for the exiled and the hunted. Those freed from concentration camps and those in distant Russian exile had the choice of returning to their former homes. Some did so, often only to discover that those who had benefited from Nazi rule by appropriating the property of Jews were deeply disappointed to see the former owners come to life and claim their own. There was stubborn resistance to returning the property in question. Where there was decency in the governments of the western lands, such disputes were eventually adjusted. Things were different in the eastern countries because too many people had profited from the ruin of their Jewish neighbors. The few Jews who straggled back to Poland found no trace of family, friends, or populous Jewish community. What they did find was consuming hatred on the part of men and women who were enjoying the fruits of murder, in which they may or may not have participated, but which they certainly had done nothing to avert. The Polish clergy, charging that the returned Jews were communists—there were a few communists in the first postwar Polish government—sided with their flocks. There were numerous beatings and murders of returned Jews. The most spectacular of such assaults was the pogrom, deliberately planned and carried out, at Kielce on July 4, 1946. In every possible sense of hearth and fatherland, the returned Jews were now homeless. There was a renewed flight, this time westward into the displaced persons' camps under American and British control.

The displaced persons' camps remained in the news for several years after the war. They were maintained at great expense to the government and to the Jews of the United States. It seemed impossible to dispose of the few score thousands who were practically all that remained of formerly great Jewish communities. The restrictive immigration laws of the United States remained in force, and the west European countries also shut their gates in the face of the DP's. The rate at which homes were found for them was so slow that it looked as though the camps would become permanent monuments to Nazism and to human heartlessness in general. There was, of course, an obvious solution, namely, to transport the DP's to Palestine. That, in fact, was where the majority of them preferred to go, and there were hundreds, perhaps thousands, who were aided by Palestinian Jews in smuggling themselves into the country. But no large-scale immigration was permitted: the British barred the way.

3. A NATION IS REBORN

The key to events of the next few years is the fact that Palestinian Jews—both those who had labored for more than a generation to make the stony land a home for their people, and those who had but recently passed through the European inferno—were not disposed to be pawns in Britain's, or any other country's, imperial politics. The days of *havlagah*, as uselessly practiced in the 1930's, were also at an end; nonresistance to attacks had failed to impress either the Arabs or the British. When the fighting against the Germans was over, the Jews of Palestine strengthened the Haganah, their military defense organization, which the Arab marauders feared and the British army tried to suppress. Jews everywhere felt completely justified in demanding that the inhabitants of the DP camps be transferred to Palestine, while units of the British navy used force to prevent the debarkation of those who succeeded in approaching the Palestinian shore.

World opinion, and especially opinion in the United States, compelled Britain to do something in self-justification. Toward the end of 1945 the British government consented to have the situation looked into by a joint commission of Britons and Americans. After taking evidence in the DP camps and in Palestine, the commission unanimously recommended the immediate admittance of 100,000 DP's to Palestine. But the boorish Ernest Bevin, then foreign minister of Britain, growled his refusal. Naturally, the Jews of Palestine intensified their efforts to thwart the British forces. What the British called rebellion, the Jews called defense of their human right to receive into their homes their unfortunate brethren, whom western civilization was treating as pariahs. To make matters worse, a group of extremists came into being and acted on the principle that the best defense is offense. Rejecting the mild, purely defensive policy of the Haganah as one that left the initiative in the hands of the British, this group, which called itself Irgun Tzvai Leumi (National Military Organization), under the leadership of Menahem Beigin, did not hesitate to use terrorism when it was felt that the occasion required it. The exasperated British put themselves further in the wrong by attacking the ship *Exodus 1947,* imprisoning its 4,500 DP passengers, and later forcibly transporting them back to camp in Germany.

The *Exodus* incident occurred at the very time an international commission appointed by the United Nations General Assembly was making still another effort to solve the problem of Palestine and the Jews. Britain had itself placed the matter in the hands of the United Nations and had announced at the same time that it would relinquish its mandate and evacuate the country by August 1, 1948. The General Assembly then appointed representatives of the following states to seek a solution: Australia, Canada, Czechoslovakia, Guatemala, India, Iran, the Netherlands, Peru, Sweden, Uruguay and Yugoslavia. These representatives did not find it possible to separate the problem of the DP's from the problem of Palestine. Their decision that Palestine be divided between the Jews and the Arabs was probably less an admission of Jewish achievements in Palestine than of what Christian civilization had done and was doing to the Jews: there literally was no other solution. The United Nations Commission further recommended that Jerusalem be turned into an international city, because of its sacredness to Christianity, Islam, and Judaism. On November 29, 1947, the General Assembly adopted this proposal.

The reactions of the three participants in the ongoing conflict were instructive. Britain sulked. The Arabs screamed. The Jews rejoiced. The promise of an independent Jewish state had been made by a large majority of the nations of the world, and that state would serve as a home for their fellow Jews wherever they were distressed and persecuted.

Britain did more than prepare to give up the mandate; it relinquished Palestine with unseemly haste. With all their proud traditions of fair play, too many Britons in the Palestinian army and government openly and secretly favored the Arab attackers and interfered with the Jewish defenders. Supplies and even arms seemed to be deliberately abandoned where the Arabs would find them. But if this policy was meant to discourage, frighten, and disorganize the Jews, it failed of its purpose; the results were quite the opposite. A government had, in effect, been functioning within the *Yishuv*. As the British let go, the National Commission took hold, and the entire Jewish population cooperated. Every border of the Holy Land was now alive with Arab armies ready to invade as soon as the British left, and gleefully promising to drive the Jews into the sea.

There was something tragic about the British retreat. One cannot help contrasting it with the glorious promise of those other days, in 1917, when, having issued the Balfour Declaration, Britain stood forth as the friend of the Jewish people, as the successor to Cyrus of old in sponsoring the restoration of the Jewish commonwealth. Barely thirty years later, the failure of that promise was being signalized by a decision that amounted to a rebuke by the international community, by the relinquishment of the charge once proudly assumed, by the abandonment of the country to the ravages of internal and external war. To be sure, Britain was leaving a lasting impression on the country: in the roads it had built, in the foundations of civil law it had laid, in the numerous administrative institutions it had developed as a result of its long imperial experience. And yet, all these, and many other assets it had created during its rule, would have vanished had the impending conflict been won by the side that Britain was encouraging by its untimely departure from the scene. The results of thirty years of British labor in co-operation with the Jews—the only ones who ever did co-operate—would in all probability have been wiped off the face of the earth, and the country would have been reduced to that same picturesque wilderness which it had been before Jewish vitality and creativeness had touched it with life, had the Jews not surprised the world by their successful defense.

On Friday afternoon, May 14, 1948, in the all-Jewish city of Tel Aviv, a small group of men and women who had been the leaders of the *Yishuv* met at the municipal museum and heard David Ben-Gurion solemnly proclaim the existence of the State of Israel. He recalled the age-old connection between that land and the Jewish people; he reminded the world of the hopes and efforts that had built the community; and he based the Jewish claim to the land on the vote of the United Nations the preceding November. Thus, the Jewish commonwealth, for the third time in a period of some three thousand and five hundred years, was reborn.

At that very moment, however, the new state was being invaded by several armies vowing its extinction. The Egyptians came from the south, and the Syrians from the north; the well-trained and excellently equipped Jordanian Arab Legion, under British officers, struck across the eastern boundary; Arabs within the state came forward with armies of their own. None among the Arab peoples, and few elsewhere, believed the fighting that followed could end in anything but the defeat of Israel. With a population of only 600,000, a tiny fraction of that of its enemy countries, its territory minute and wide open on three sides, its impromptu army ill-equipped, its military leadership of unproved ability, Jewish Palestine appeared to be facing obliteration. Yet, in a matter of weeks, the Israelis were driving their enemies before them, and had not the United Nations intervened and imposed a truce, would have invaded both Syria and Egypt.

The usual explanation for this unexpected outcome has noted, on the one hand, the overconfidence of the Arabs and their extremely poor leadership, and on the other, the high morale of the Jews and the superb generalship of their youthful commanders. But this cannot be the whole explanation; the morale itself has to be explained, as well as the sudden emergence of courageous and intelligent leaders. The explanation for these phenomena must be sought not only in the nature of the Zionist ideal and in the recent tragedies that had overwhelmed the people but also in the moral and intellectual history of the Jews for centuries past. Now, in freedom of body and spirit, the full vitality of the Jewish people could at last assert itself.

Unfortunately, this vitality had to manifest itself first in war, as though to bring to pass, in a different sense from that intended, an ancient prediction included in the prayers for the Ninth of Ab: "For Thou, O Lord, hast consumed it [Jerusalem] by fire, and by fire art Thou destined to rebuild it." Let it be remembered that neither the Zionist ideal nor its program had envisaged conquest. Herzl had worked for an international charter. The settlers in Palestine had acquired almost every inch of the soil they worked by purchase. Many of the Jews of Palestine had felt that they were not yet ready for independent statehood. But they were given no choice. War was forced upon them. Thousands of young men and women, who might have helped build the nation, lost their lives in its preservation.

Arab leaders urged the Palestinian Arabs to abandon

their homes, promising them that they would soon return in triumph and take possession of the property of the Jews, who would certainly be annihilated. The Arabs either heeded this advice or were compelled to heed it. In many instances, Jews pleaded with their Arab neighbors to stay; but there was no stopping the mad flight. Tens of thousands left their homes and crowded to the borders of Syria, Egypt, Jordan, and Lebanon in the hope of a quick, safe, and profitable return.

The United Nations was in the meantime trying to effect an armistice between Israel and the Arab nations. It became easier to achieve this as the months rolled by and the Arabs lost their enthusiasm for fighting the Israelis. The United Nations had appointed Count Folke Bernadotte, of Sweden, the chairman of the International Red Cross and a well-meaning diplomat, as chief mediator between the two sides. It became known that Count Bernadotte, perhaps under British influence, was about to use his prestige and his powers to impose on Israel terms that would have drastically restricted the territory under its control. Some Israeli terrorists thereupon assassinated him. It was shocking evidence of the war's effect on morals, and no one was more disturbed by this act than the Jews of Israel and of the diaspora. The United Nations efforts did not slacken, however; Dr. Ralph Bunche of the United States became the mediator, and a truce was arranged.

The temporary boundaries of Israel were drawn largely in terms of the lines held at the cessation of fighting. It came about that the lines of demarcation were not easy to follow, that Egyptian and Jordanian territory cut deep into that held by Israel, and most striking of all, that the city of Jerusalem was split in two: the old city, having been overrun by the Arab Legion, was left in Jordanian hands; the new city in the hands of Israel. A deplorable result of the truce was that the area of Mount Scopus, with its Hadassah hospital and the valuable buildings and library of the Hebrew University, likewise fell to Jordan.

For the time being, the important consideration was that Israel existed. The first country to recognize this fact was the United States, President Harry S. Truman having announced his government's recognition of Israel within hours after Israel's proclamation of independence. Other governments followed rapidly. Within a year, fifty-four states had done so, forty-five of these being members of the United Nations. On May 11, 1949, Israel itself was admitted to the international body. This event did not mean, of course, that even its territorial status was settled. The fighting had seriously upset the boundaries fixed by the United Nations in its resolution of November 1947.

There was, moreover, the difficult question of Jerusalem's status. Originally, it was planned to make Jerusalem a separate entity ruled by an international authority, because of the location within its area of the places sacred to Christians, Moslems, and Jews. Actually, such an arrangement would have proved impractical. Jordan objected to it far more than did Israel, which pointed out that of the thirty or so sacred sites in Jerusalem, only two were within the new city and therefore under Jewish control. Many Christians agreed that a Jewish state that did not include Jerusalem would be highly incongruous. Nevertheless, the United Nations refused to modify its original vote on the subject, perhaps because of the opposition of those nations that were influenced by the views of the Catholic Church. In 1953 the Israel government moved all its offices to Jerusalem, which was declared, thenceforth, the capital of the state. Several governments, however, refused to recognize the validity of the move.

4. THE PROBLEMS OF THE NEW STATE

Since the immediate motivation for the establishment of the state was the need of the homeless Jews, it was inevitable that its doors should be thrown wide open to all who wished to come. The first arrivals were those Jews whom Britain had intercepted during the closing days of the mandate and had kept in its own DP camps on the island of Cyprus. Simultaneously, the camps in Europe began to be emptied of those who had looked longingly toward the Promised Land. Moreover, in the bitterness of defeat, the Arab nations, those directly concerned as well as others, aggravated the problems of Israel by making life intolerable for the Jews in their lands, so that large numbers, leaving their property behind, escaped to Israel. Scores of thousands came from North Africa and western Asia. The most colorful group of these new immigrants were the simple, pious, hard-working Yemenite Jews. Under the protection of Great Britain, they made their way overland to Aden and thence were transported by air to Israel. For westerners this relocation was called "Operation Magic Carpet"; for the Yemenites themselves it was the fulfillment of the divine promise made through Isaiah that they would "mount up with wings as eagles" (Isaiah 40:31).

The arrival of so many immigrants all at once naturally intensified and complicated Israel's economic and social problems. The country was not producing enough for its vastly increased population, while the boycott by its neighbors permitted no expansion of foreign trade. Consequently, the support of the new population called for measures as heroic as those that had brought the state into being. The older residents had to ration their food in order to feed the newcomers. A vast retraining program had to be undertaken to fit the able-bodied among the immigrants into their new life. Large numbers had to be housed temporarily in transition camps (ma'abarot).

As for the Arab refugees from Israel, none of the Arab countries, despite their great size and sparse populations, was willing to do for its fellow Arabs what the Israelis were doing for their fellow Jews. Nothing of the enormous profits from the rich oil lands was given for refugee support. The Arab nations did not, in fact, want the problem solved at all. They insisted that Israel permit the former inhabitants to return. They knew very well that this step, if taken, would make the functioning of the new state impossible both economically and politically and would endanger its security. There were already about 150,000 Arabs in Israel who had ignored the advice of the Arab leaders that they leave and had remained to become part of the new state. In time, Israel admitted many thousands more, so that families might be reunited. Compensation was offered for the property of others. The United States offered to finance large-scale irrigation projects in the Arab lands; Arab soil, thus made more fertile, would be able to absorb the homeless. Eric Johnston, the American emissary, tried on several occasions to point out the great advantages of such a plan. However, since its undoubted success would remove their best propaganda weapon against Israel, the Arabs turned it down. The refugees had, in fact, become a weapon in the war of the Moslem nations against Israel. The former continued to insist that they would not discuss peace until the refugees were readmitted to Israel. Israel's answer has been that the problem of the refugees was an item for the agenda in the discussions of peace, not a precondition for it. In the meantime, some 750,000 human beings—the number of refugees grew naturally, and by the attraction from the other Arab nations of elements seeking free support—have been maintained by the United Nations.

The Jewish population of Israel rose from about 600,000 immediately after World War II to more than 2,000,000 in 1959. The statistics for 1958 indicated 1,780,000 Jews, 147,000 Moslems, 45,000 (mostly Arab) Christians, and 21,000 Druse. By that year 914,000 immigrants had come to settle in Israel. Put differently, this means that, exclusive of the children born during the 1950's, over fifty per cent of its people have lived in the country less than a decade. What is more, these people differ from one another as Europeans differ from Asians and Africans, as the German Jew differs from the Yemenite and all shades in between—linguistically, economically, religiously, in color of skin, in habits of life, in outlook, and in hopes. That these different people have undertaken to fuse into one nation is evidence of the power of an idea, whether religious or historical; at the same time, this common undertaking to build a nation forces them to face a number of tremendous problems.

The problem of languages has been solved: Hebrew remains the uncontested language of the country. It has, indeed, experienced a renaissance, growing in vocabulary and increasing in suppleness to meet every modern need. As one would expect, much of the literature produced for Israel's highly literate population still deals with the period of diaspora upheaval and immigration; but the stronger trend is clearly toward the experience of the Israel war and of cultural readjustment.

Compulsory, universal schooling must in time succeed in giving the population a basic cultural unity. So too, universal military training for men and women was so organized as to serve not only national defense, but also as a force in overcoming the differences arising from environmental backgrounds. Under the influence of that part of Israel's population which hails from Europe, the entire people was certain to remain culturally sensitive. Newspapers, books, museums, symphony orchestras, and other appeals to mind and heart have aimed at achieving unity without external compulsion. But the problems that go deeper into the human spirit are not so easily solved.

Idealism and intelligence have worked wonders, but economic factors cannot be left out of consideration. The proportionately tremendous immigration multiplied the difficulties of the new state. How to increase the productivity of the soil had been a problem ever since the days of the First Aliyah. The need to achieve this was now made the more urgent in order to feed the newcomers. Since imports had to be kept to a minimum, the population of older residence consented to rationing of food for a number of years. In a more positive sense, apart from the rapid planting of more agricultural colonies, industries had to be established and many of the immigrants trained to do the sort of work to which they had not been accustomed. The boycott tightly maintained by the Arab states surrounding Israel further restricted the possibilities of balancing the national budget. Between 1952 and 1954 Israel reluctantly yielded to the necessity of reducing the rate of immigration. But in 1955 the Jews of several North African states had to be granted refuge from conditions in that part of the world. Finally, all through the years since its establishment, Israel had to make great expenditures for defense.

Progress made despite these difficulties has been astonishing. It has included the draining of swamps and opening new land to cultivation, the stretching of water pipelines into the Negev, the building of roads, especially that to Beersheba and Sodom, the establishing of factories, and the introduction of new industries. The foundations have been laid for a merchant fleet. The oil discovered in the Negev has thus far been limited in quantity, but it promises to increase. Though imports fell off in the course of the state's first decade, and exports rose, there was still a substantial imbalance of trade. This has been made up by bond sales, contributions, and investments on the part of the Jews of the diaspora, and to some extent, by limited and decreasing extensions of credit by the United States and other governments. The German reparation funds must also be considered in this connection.

One of the most serious problems for a state like Israel is, naturally, that of religion. The Moslems and the members of Christian denominations in Israel are, of course, unaffected by religious controversy among the Jews. Within the Jewish community, however, differences of religion range from atheism to the extremest type of Orthodoxy. Continuing the policies of the British, the Israel government has operated with an organized religious community. There is a chief rabbinate; marriage and divorce are impossible without religious ceremonial; the army and other government institutions observe Jewish traditions in *kashrut* and the like. But the extremist religious forces cannot be satisfied with these concessions; they hold that Judaism must pervade all of life. On this theory, the government would have to enforce *kashrut* and Sabbath observance on everyone. On the other hand, large segments of the population are equally convinced of the need to separate religion from the state. They would even discontinue those connections with Judaism that have obtained until now, letting religion remain, as in western states, a matter for the individual's conscience to decide. The battle has been postponed, but the differences are still unresolved. Sooner or later, Israel will have to decide, in democratic fashion, what its future religious policy is to be, and that decision must, in the very nature of things, affect the Judaism of the diaspora.

It may have been fear of just such a disruptive argument, while the state was still weak, that caused the adjournment of debate on a constitution. For a commission to draw one up was appointed soon after the state was established. Eventually, articles were formulated and brought forward for discussion, but it was felt that the time for adopting a constitution had not yet come. More experience of actual government and more crystallization of ideals were needed before definite regulations could be adopted. For the Jews of Israel are fully aware that a basic law formulated by them must express the Jewish spirit at its best and Jewish experience at its noblest. The law that prevails pending the adoption of a constitution is therefore a mixture of Jewish civil and ethical law and British common law. A judiciary functions with a supreme court at its head. A president is elected by the Knesset, the one-chamber legislature. His position is more decorative and unifying, like that of the sovereigns of Britain, than possessed of authority like that of the president of the United States. The actual government is vested in a cabinet and its prime minister responsible to the Knesset, very much like the arrangement in Great Britain and other European countries. Elections are held every four years, or more often if the cabinet finds that it no longer has the support of a majority of the Knesset but feels that it does have the support of the majority of the population.

The first eleven years of the state's existence witnessed four elections: January 25, 1949, June 30, 1951, November 26, 1955, November 3, 1959. In all four, Mapai, the moderate socialist party, received the largest number of votes. In the first two, the socialists farther to the left, who bear the name Mapam, came next; and the religious forces third. Herut, the economically more conservative and politically more activist party, showed gains in the third and fourth elections. The fourth election was distinguished by the participation of more than double the number of voters in the first (1,200,000 as against 500,000). Attempts to capitalize on the dissatisfaction of groups of various racial origins failed; even the North African Jews, whose complaints had been the loudest, integrated themselves into the existing party system. Of the 120 members in the Knesset, Mapai retained the largest representation, forty-seven, a gain of seven; Mapam remained practically unchanged; the General Zionists, representing the middle and upper economic groups, won only eight seats, a loss of five; the religious parties gained slightly; Herut won two additional seats, now having seventeen, while the communists lost three of the six they had held. Every Knesset has had from three to five Arab members.

About a dozen different parties are represented in the Knesset; still others received such small numbers of votes as to have earned no representation at all, since the system followed is that of proportional representation. In view of the large number of parties and of the fact that none received a majority in any election, the government has had to consist of a coalition of parties. The cabinet, like the Knesset, has represented a balance of power reflecting the balance of opinion in the population. Thus, in every possible way, Israel has attempted to practice the maximum of political democracy.

The first president of Israel was the veteran leader of Zionism, Dr. Chaim Weizmann. Upon his death, in 1952, the choice of the Knesset fell on the unpretentious, popular, scholarly Yitzhak Ben-Zvi, who had come to Palestine in 1907 with the Second Aliyah; he was re-elected in 1957 for a second term of five years. The able and dynamic leader, David Ben-Gurion, who had settled in Palestine in 1906, and who had stood at the head of the *Yishuv*'s government during the latter days of the British mandate, was again entrusted with the prime ministry. For a while, in 1954 and 1955, he relinquished his post to his colleague Moshe Sharett, the first foreign secretary of Israel, and retired to a small settlement in the Negev. But when the situation became critical for Israel, Ben-Gurion resumed his former office (November 1955), while the foreign ministry was taken over by Golda Meir (Meyerson), who had been a member of the Israel government from the beginning.

The ability of Israel to solve its internal problems has not extended to the difficult situation that it confronts in the unabated hostility of its neighbors. As so frequently in the past of the Jewish people, Israel has found itself in the midst of a world crisis. The awakening nationalism of peoples hitherto considered colonies of western nations has brought political revolution to the Middle East. From the very beginning of the Jewish migration to Palestine, the Arabs looked upon the immigrating Jews as representatives of western culture and therefore as part of the colonizing movement—more of the colonizers who had in the past despised and dominated them. The Arabs had refused to believe the claims of the Jews that they were returning "home." They had had little interest in the refusal of the Jewish labor unions to countenance the reduction of Arabs to the position of serfdom. They had suspected and refused to co-operate when in the 1930's and 1940's, under the leadership of Judah L. Magnes and other idealists, they were besought to join the Jews on the basis of union and equality. The state of Israel was thus clearly expiating the sins of the western colonizing powers, of those very states some of which were now assuming an attitude of self-righteousness, and sympathizing with the Arabs. Moreover, it suited the politics of Russia to utilize the state of affairs in the Middle East to reduce the influence of the United States and other nations of the west. At the same time, powerful diplomatic forces in the United States, having inherited the myopia of the British Colonial Office in the prewar era along with many of its headaches, have made every effort to retain influence in the Moslem world. Both of these world problems, Arab nationalism and the East-West conflict, have militated against the establishment of peace between Israel and its neighbors.

Defeated in the war of 1948, the Arab nations embarked upon a guerrilla fight. Hardly a day passed without some hit-and-run attack on the Jewish colonies along the borders, or on Israel army patrols. The United Nations Armistice Commission, stationed in Israel and in the Arab lands to adjudge such cases and condemn the guilty, defined its task as preventing retaliatory action as well as attack. The Arab nations, which loudly proclaimed their intention to avenge their defeat in a "second round," succeeded after 1955 in obtaining large consignments of arms from communist countries. With the exception of France, the western nations were, on the other hand, unwilling to sell or grant arms to Israel. Under such conditions, the prospects for peace were dimmed considerably.

In the last days of October 1956, Israel, aware of the vast preparations made by the Egyptian dictator Gamal Abdel Nasser to invade and destroy it, and unable to tolerate any longer the unceasing incursions of Egyptian murder bands, sent its army into the Gaza strip and the Sinai Peninsula to destroy the bases from which the attacks were being launched. These objectives were won within a week. The French and the British also attacked, seeking to regain control of the Suez Canal, which Egypt had nationalized contrary to international understanding. But the United States and the United Nations demanded that France and Britain withdraw and again interpreted Israel's act of self-defense as aggression. Israel thereupon agreed to withdraw its forces from Sinai. It made the withdrawal contingent, however, on the United Nations preventing Egypt from reoccupying the Gaza Strip and the entrance to the Gulf of Aqaba. But no sooner had Israel withdrawn than the United Nations as well as the United States went back on the spirit, if not the letter, of the understanding. Egyptian forces reoccupied both Sinai and Gaza, and only the international patrol on the border, organized and maintained by the United Nations, prevented the resumption of the Egyptian marauding expeditions. The one gain for Israel was its ability to use the Bay of Aqaba to and from the port of Elath, although Saudi Arabia continued to protest that this was somehow a danger to it and to the pilgrims to Mecca. On the other hand, the United Nations did nothing at all when Nasser of Egypt expelled, and confiscated the property of, thousands of Jews whose families had lived in Egypt for generations and had carried on business there.

A further complication in the intricate politics of the Middle East was due to Egypt's use of nascent Arab nationalism to dominate the entire area. Enmity against Israel was the one emotion common to all Moslem states and therefore proved to be Colonel Nasser's most effective tool. Saved from destruction, if not from defeat, by the intervention of the United States and the United Nations, he resumed his aggressive design to make himself head of a Moslem empire. His first step toward such an empire was the absorption of Syria in a United Arab Republic. The Kingdom of Jordan being clearly due to be the next step in the expansion of Egypt's power, the threat to Israel is obvious.

Russia, eager to displace the west, especially the United States, from its position of influence in the area, continued to give Egypt armaments as well as diplomatic support. That the primary goal was not Israel's destruction but rather the extension of Egyptian power became clear in July 1958 when revolutionary uprisings were fomented in Iraq and Lebanon. American and British troops had to intervene in order to maintain the west's prestige and its oil concessions. Thwarted in this respect, Nasser fell back on his anti-Israel position and again sought to stand out as the foremost defender of this Arab cause. In defiance of the United Nations and in violation of his clearly given promise to keep the Suez Canal open to all shipping, he refused to permit any ship, of whatever nation, to pass through the canal if it had stopped at an Israel port. The Arab nations, moreover, intensified their boycott of Israel by trying to spread it among the business and shipping interests of the western nations.

On the fifth of Iyar, April 25, 1958, Israel celebrated the tenth anniversary of its statehood. There was a military parade in Jerusalem; but more important, there was undiminished hope and faith in the hearts of its people. Much had been achieved in the ten years, but the basic aim of peace was still far off.

VI

. . . .

The Diaspora After World War II

. . . .

1. ANTI-SEMITISM AND THE SEARCH FOR UNITY IN THE UNITED STATES

Not the least important result of the establishment of Israel as an independent state was its effect on the diaspora. With a mixture of pride and hope, Jews greeted this evidence of the unexhausted vitality of their brethren. Participants in Jewish life were elated. Even those who had become quite alien to any manifestation of Judaism, who had apparently long since succumbed to the cultural pull of the environment, now again expressed interest in Jewish fate. In the United States, however, a small group of those who had always been anti-Zionist voiced loud objection. They called themselves the American Council for Judaism; in point of fact, their energies were directed against Zionism and against support for the Jewish state. With this small exception, the Jews of the diaspora found new unity in their enthusiasm for the state that, in addition to its appeal to heart and mind, offered some consolation for the pain and despair experienced while Nazism was in the ascendant in Europe and anti-Semitism in the United States.

Israel apart, the diaspora communities, especially that of the United States, after World War II, faced once more the problems of adjustment and survival. A new generation, the second or third of even the east European migration, had by this time taken control. Intellectually and economically this generation did not feel the cleavage with Jews of different origins as keenly as had its parents. Moreover, comparatively few immigrants had entered the United States since the restrictive immigration laws had come into force. Those from central Europe fitted themselves easily into the pattern of American Jewish life. Many of those who brought traditions from more eastern districts of Europe contributed some interesting and important variations to the pattern. But they had practically no influence as yet on the perennial Jewish diaspora problem of how to articulate the fears and hopes of the Jewish population.

Community organization had taken considerable steps forward during the war. This was so of necessity, since work of rescue and relief was an obligation that American Jews never dodged. The magnificent aid extended to Israel during its life-struggle strengthened the local community organizations. But they remained largely fund-raising rather than functional bodies. Voices were raised occasionally in behalf of some form of representative local community agency. None of the larger communities, however, responded to any such call, and the characteristic basis of American community life remained philanthropy combined with defense. There were, indeed, important leaders of Jewish thought who argued that in the free environment of western democracy, no other basis was possible or even desirable. To attack such nation-wide problems as affected all the local federations, the Council of Jewish Federations and Welfare Funds had been organized in 1932. Its functions being primarily those of research and consultation, the Council was obviously not the body to represent the Jewish population of the United States.

A paradoxical notion, widely entertained by Jews the world over, is that anti-Semitism somehow has helped Jewish survival. The fact of survival during the many centuries of oppression lends countenance to the assumption that the enemies of the Jews have kept them alive. It is true that as the tide of anti-Jewishness rose in England or America or anywhere else, Jews flocked to the support of defense organizations. It was an understandable reaction on the part of decent men. But this natural defensive attitude has given the false impression of staunch loyalty. It was rarely anything of the sort. It added much to the suspicions with which Jews regarded their neighbors, but it implied no commitment to Judaism or to the Jewish people. It intensified the Jewish sense of insecurity, of not belonging to the majority, but it also made for impatience with all those elements of Jewish life that differentiated Judaism from the surrounding civilization. It thus made for a psychology of escape, of intermarriage, and of denial of self. An attitude prevailed that tested every word and deed, every book and undertaking, not by its effectiveness in strengthening Judaism and the Jewish community, but by the impression it was likely to make on Christian neighbors. Another result of this aspect of Jewish experience during the fourth and fifth decades of the century was a stronger conviction among those already firm in their Jewishness that little mercy and less love were to be found among many of those who use these terms continuously; it also made some alienated Jews look back to their origins.

The greater organizational unity that might have been expected from concentration on defense did not result from it. During World War II a proposal was advanced that the Jews of the United States organize a body that would be representative of them all and thus concentrate their influence on improving the situation of Jews the world over when the time came for negotiating the peace. The characteristic counterargument during the discussion of this proposal was based on the fear that any such attempt at unity would be misunderstood by the rest of the country's population. Finally, the idea was accepted, and the American Jewish Conference was organized. It held a preliminary meeting in Pittsburgh in January 1943, and its first regular session, in New York, August 29 to September 2 of the same year. Although a number of factors inherent in the situation prevented the Conference from leading anything but a shadowy existence, it served a useful purpose in providing a broad Zionist and non-Zionist front in behalf of the idea of a Jewish commonwealth in Palestine. It also dealt with several other matters of concern to the American Jewish Community. In January 1949 the Conference decided to discontinue its labors.

If the disbanding of the Conference was justified on the ground that its work overlapped the programs of other existing organizations, the same argument could be applied to the ongoing and expanding activities of the various defense agencies. The American Jewish Committee, the American Jewish Congress, the Anti-Defamation League of the B'nai B'rith, the Jewish Labor Committee, and the local and regional Jewish Community Relations Councils that had come into existence during the 1930's and had since organized a National Community Relations Advisory Council —all of these, and others, were engaged in more or less the same type of work. Yielding to common sense, and under some pressure from the communal fund-raising organizations, these agencies agreed in 1950 to invite Professor Robert M. MacIver, a noted sociologist, to evaluate their total effort and to submit his recommendations. In his report in 1951, while recognizing the worthwhileness of Jewish defense work both for the Jewish group and for American democracy in general, Dr. MacIver advised that defense could be made more effective and efficient if various aspects of the work were done by organizations specializing in them and if authority to assign tasks were placed in the National Community Relations Advisory Council. These recommendations did not fall pleasantly on the ears of some of the organizations involved; in particular, some of the more influential and well-established among them felt that their very reason for existence was being questioned. Following heated discussion and much negotiation, the American Jewish Committee and the Anti-Defamation League declined to join in the implementation of Dr. MacIver's recommendations. These organizations stood by the view that various elements of the Jewish population had a democratic right to combat anti-Semitism in their own way and that unity was therefore neither necessary nor desirable.

Actually, however, the interest of the Jews veered away from anti-Semitism to a considerable degree after World War II. In the United States, the upward swing of economic life, the proved connection between anti-Jewishness and Nazi as well as communist antidemocracy, and the obviously irrational and self-seeking character of the known anti-Jewish agitators led most non-Jews to turn a deaf ear to the wild charges that the professional hate-spreaders continued to mouth. There was, moreover, a marked improvement in the presentation of Jews and Judaism in popular fiction and in the periodical press. Nevertheless, even the 1950's were not completely free from evidences of hostility. Racialist prejudices manifested themselves in 1952, when Congress passed, over President Truman's veto, the McCarran-Walter Act, which retained, and in some instances intensified, existing restrictions on the immigration of presumed non-Nordics. A well-financed attempt to rearouse anti-Semitism was made during the same decade, when the old-fashioned anti-Semite was joined and supported by Arab and pro-Arab propagandists trying to frighten American Jews away from aiding Israel and to promote a public opinion adverse to the new state. Still another source of danger was the Negroes' struggle for educational and social equality, which created a reactionary atmosphere in the Southern part of the United States. It resulted in some intimidation of Jews and in the bombing of several synagogues. A rash of synagogue swastika-daubings broke out even in the North in the last days of 1959. A portion of the population had not given up its attitude of suspicion toward the Jewish minority.

On the whole, however, the situation improved noticeably. There are issues on which Jews and Christians do not see eye to eye—the teaching of religion in the public schools, for example—and which can be utilized by demagogues to create a major storm. But, given continuous peace and prosperity such demagogues can meet with little success. With the Jews no longer under direct attack, defense organizations learned to join their efforts to the general striving for economic stability, social progress, and equality of rights for all minorities. The fight against anti-Semitism ceased to be as spectacular and as urgent as it used to be, and the attention of the Jewish people could be turned to more deep-seated problems and to creative tasks.

2. READJUSTMENT IN POSTWAR EUROPE

A similar decrease in active anti-Semitism could be noted in most other parts of the world in the early 1950's. The most dramatic development was the official acknowledgment by Germany of guilt for what had happened to the Jews during the Nazi era. The West German government agreed to negotiate with representatives of Israel and of the diaspora Jewish communities on the subject of material indemnification for what Jews had suffered. It was not easy for Jews to enter into negotiations with Germany; it looked to some like willingness to be satisfied with money as compensation for so many lives and so much suffering. Clearly, however, it could never become a matter of forgiveness or being forgiven for willful murder or complicity in it. What was at stake here was not reparation for the slaughtered millions, but on the one side, an expression of regret, and on the other, acceptance of aid for those who had suffered and for the descendants of those who had died. Chancellor Konrad Adenauer's government had, indeed, voiced this very attitude when, on September 27, 1951, it had submitted the following resolution to the West German Parliament in Bonn:

> The Federal Government is prepared, jointly with the representatives of Jewry and the State of Israel which has admitted so many homeless Jewish refugees, to bring about a solution of the material reparations problem in order to facilitate the way to a spiritual purging of unheard-of suffering.

When this resolution was read, the representatives of Germany rose in unanimous acceptance. This memory-laden moment should not be forgotten.

Agreement between West Germany and the Jewish representatives was reached on September 10, 1952. West Germany agreed to pay Israel $715,000,000 worth of goods and to give an additional $107,000,000 to the Conference on Jewish Material Claims against Germany for indemnification to persons who had suffered under or lost property in Nazi Germany. The payments were to be made over a period of nine years. As a result, Israel was able within the next few years to draw upon Germany for a considerable amount of essential machinery and to add to its commercial and passenger shipping. Some writers and scholars, moreover, both in Israel and the diaspora, could be granted support while working on a variety of cultural contributions. Similar negotiations with Austria did not have such a satisfactory outcome. The Austrian government proved less sensitive to shame for its people's past. It dragged out the negotiations until the western governments, in the Austrian peace treaty of 1955, urged greater responsiveness. By 1960 Austria had passed legislation covering only about five per cent of the total losses suffered by its former Jewish inhabitants, and no real settlement appeared in sight.

Clearly, anti-Semitism in Europe in the 1950's did not speak in the strident tones it had used in previous decades; but it had not disappeared. Time and again voices were heard in Germany repeating the arrogant and bloodthirsty claims of Nazism, sometimes granting that Hitler had made mistakes, but usually merely regretting his defeat. The considerable number of former Nazis promoted to positions of influence was equally disturbing. It was revealed in 1959 that German schools taught nothing about the Hitler era, thereby presumably failing to arouse the conscience of the next generation to guard against a revival of the extreme nationalism and brutality of the past. Such fears were intensified when, late in 1959, the bombing of the newly-built synagogue in Munich by members of a neo-Nazi group led to similar desecrations of Jewish institutions in other parts of the world. Such sentiments and actions did not represent official Germany and probably did not represent the large majority of Germans; but they did not represent them in the 1920's either.

The Jews of Germany, though well established materially, were by 1960 still too small in number—fewer than 40,000 in the Bonn republic—to serve as a test of the Germany that lived in the hearts of its people. Equally disturbing was the

appearance in France of Poujadism as a lower-class movement with distinctly fascistic and anti-Semitic tendencies.
Under its leader, Pierre Poujade, it polled a considerable
popular vote in the elections of January 1956. Yet this did
not stand in the way of France's showing sympathy for Israel
during and since the Suez incident. Moreover, Poujadism
sank out of sight when the De Gaulle government took over
in France. In Great Britain, Sir Oswald Mosley and his Union Movement occasionally broke into the news during the
1950's. In other European countries similar manifestations
occurred from time to time. In fact, an international union
of anti-Semites had several meetings during the early 1950's.
They appeared to have no influence, however, on the peoples
and governments of Europe west of the communist bloc.

To find really flagrant evidences of anti-Semitism in contemporary Europe, one must peep behind the Iron Curtain.
Although the Soviet Union has continued to pride itself on
having declared anti-Semitism illegal, evidences of it have
cropped up repeatedly. During the last years of Stalin's life,
he showed himself increasingly intolerant of Jews and Jewish culture. The frequency with which the charge of "root-
less cosmopolitanism"—whatever the phrase meant—was
leveled against people bearing Jewish names could not have
been accidental. In 1948 practically all Jewish writers were
arrested and deported to Siberia. The so-called "Doctors'
Plot" in 1952, in which it was charged that prominent phy-
sicians—most of them Jews—had planned to kill the leaders
of the Soviet Union, was clearly the opening move of an
old-fashioned anti-Semitic campaign. The death of Stalin,
in March 1953, and the subsequent eclipse and execution of
Lavrenti Beria brought the campaign against the Jews to a
halt. Some of the deported writers returned from Siberian
exile; here and there a Yiddish theater was permitted to re-
open. But a Yiddish press worthy of the name no longer
existed, and Yiddish schools remained closed.

American rabbis who visited Russia in 1956 thought that
they sensed a hunger for religion among the Jews, but they

could see little chance for that hunger to be satisfied. To be sure, no stigma attached to identifying oneself as of Jewish origin. The fields of science and scholarship did not exclude Jews, though leadership in other areas, including the military, was restricted. The determination to have done with a distinct Jewish people and culture is obvious. The older generation is to be permitted to die out in comparative peace. Without schools, without books, without adequate leadership, without even functionaries to perform the minor religious duties, no new generation can arise. Nor will Russia permit emigration to Israel, since that would displease the Arab states. It is a punishable offense in Russia for Jews to possess Zionist literature. In reaction to widespread criticism of this effort to stifle an ancient culture and religion, the Soviet government permitted the reprinting of a Hebrew prayer book—the first since the communist revolution —and issued in 1959 a thin collection of Shalom Aleichem stories in Yiddish to honor the centennial of his birth.

The other communist-dominated states in eastern Europe have shown not the least interest in absorbing their Jewish populations. If not for Russian objections, these states would probably have encouraged their Jewish inhabitants to emigrate to Israel. Since they must, for the time being, follow Moscow's dictates, these states have held back the Jews, though in several instances they have permitted Jewish religious and communal life to continue. Their governments have discouraged anti-Semitic manifestations, though on occasion these governments themselves have not been above talking in anti-Jewish terms.

The Jews of Poland consist of those few who came out of their hiding places after the war, or returned as survivors of concentration camps, as well as a considerable number who, as Polish citizens who had found refuge in Russia, chose to come "home." The population has about it a sense of impermanence. In 1957 alone, soon after the nationalist-communist government attained power, about 30,000 Polish Jews emigrated to Israel. The Polish government reduced the rate of emigration in 1958 to about 270 a month. The 40,000 Jews remaining there in 1959 were in a bad way economically. Their agricultural collectives were not prospering. Moreover, the new government's grant of wider powers to the Church was interpreted by the Polish population as giving greater latitude to practice anti-Semitism. The result has been further limitation on the possibilities of Jewish economic adjustment. The Joint Distribution Committee has done much to help, and the Jewish American Ort has established a number of manual training centers. At the same time, Jewish community organization is possible and officially recognized. There are synagogues and schools, and there is some cultural activity. An interesting fact, which sheds some light on the Jewish situation in eastern Europe, is that in 1958 a *mohel* from America came to Poland for the purpose of circumcising a number of children who had returned from Russia.

The postwar situation in Rumania presented a few elements of contrast with that in Poland. Rumania's 225,000 Jews—compare the number with the 750,000 who lived there before the war—were permitted religious and cultural activity, and anti-Semitism was kept under control by the government. The economic situation of Rumania's Jews, however, has become increasingly sad, since the government itself, courting the favor of the masses, has indulged in economic discrimination against the Jews. Perhaps this explains why, in 1958 and early 1959, the Rumanian government suddenly embarked upon a policy of permitting emigration to Israel. Upon the complaint of the Arab states, and orders from Moscow, emigration was just as suddenly stopped.

Another glimpse into Jewish fate behind the Iron Curtain was obtained during the Hungarian revolt against communism and Russian domination in the latter part of 1956. Among those who tried desperately to cross the boundaries into Austria so as ultimately to go to the west, were many Jews. On the one hand, some of the refugee camps into which the escaped families were herded had to maintain a guard against outbreaks of anti-Semitism among those who were presumably animated by the noble sentiments of a free world. On the other hand, some Hungarian government officials since the suppression of the revolt have not hesitated to blame the tragic incident on the Jews. There is, however, a Jewish community in Hungary, and its 100,000 people enjoy a fair degree of religious and cultural freedom.

By the end of the 1950's one was faced with the strange situation that, whereas anti-Semitism continued to exist in almost every part of Europe, its manifestations were most virulent and destructive under communism. To be sure, these manifestations differed from the usual brand of anti-Jewishness in that they sought to starve the spirit rather than destroy the body. But no one would have thought this possible in the 1920's.

3. NEW TRENDS IN RELIGION

The period of adjustment and conflict left its mark on the Judaism of western Europe and America. It emerged at the end of the half century different both from the Judaism the immigrants had found on their arrival and from that which they had brought with them. A survey made in 1953 of an eastern American city with a Jewish population of several thousand may be considered representative of the Jews in the United States in general, especially of those living away from the large centers of Jewish population. Only thirty per cent of that city's Jews expressed strong objection to intermarriage, which had, indeed, risen in that community to seven per cent of all marriages in which Jews were a party. Most Jews, however, were more or less conscious of their Judaism, its culture, and its values. Having attained a degree of middle-class comfort, identifying themselves fully with American culture and civilization, the American Jews of the mid-twentieth century appear to feel but vaguely the ties binding them to Judaism and to the Jews as a group. The process of assimilation to the extent of self-forgetfulness has made visible inroads upon Jewish religious life. Jewish novelists of the post-World War II era, whether they portrayed Jewish characters of the vulgar or the more intellectual type, have also reflected this strain on Jewish survival.

Yet, far from being discouraging, the record must be considered quite good in view of the attractiveness of the majority culture and the numerous problems and difficulties the Jewish group has had to face under circumstances that made centralized control and direction impossible. That internal ties would be weakened could have been, and was, foreseen; but that so many of the third, fourth, and sometimes even later generations, should still have strong attachments to the religion and way of life of a small minority is evidence of Judaism's vigor. Those who remember the dire predictions of a generation ago must feel encouraged by the quest on the part of the younger generation, practically all native-born, for closer contacts with Jewish tradition.

A number of factors may be called upon to explain this unexpected situation. The middle years of the twentieth century witnessed a reaction against the rather cold rationalism that dominated the thought of the century's earlier years. Whatever the cause for this change in the world in general, the new intellectual climate also affected the Jews; the trend toward religion did not leave them untouched. Closely allied with this general trend was the improvement in the economic status of the Jewish population. Whereas the thinking of the parents had been largely socialist when the factory or shop was central in their lives, the children, now possessed of greater financial resources, even though equally plagued by a sense of insecurity, took on the thought-patterns of the middle class. An American Jew, as the above-mentioned survey indicates, thought of himself as primarily a member of a religious group. Moving into a suburban neighborhood, he sought social identification with fellow Jews, either out of self-respect or out of a lingering sense of insecurity. He continued neglecting his religious observances, but he joined a synagogue, especially after his children attained school age. The synagogue as an institution thus grew in prominence during and immediately after World War II, but whether it would grow in influence remained an open question.

The environmental and sociological factors now operating in the development of Judaism were more or less external; they could become positive only if the Jewish spirit upon which they impinged remained alive and functioning. In many instances the environment won by default, and the Jewishness of the Jews degenerated into mere social habit. The environment consequently did not benefit from any new and challenging viewpoint, and the Judaism of the people involved remained unaware of any spiritual or cultural challenge. It therefore became clear that nothing was more important for the maintenance of Jewish life than efforts to give meaning to Judaism and to its institutions.

Such religious discussion and interpretation had never ceased throughout the twentieth century. Jewish thought may no longer have had the uniformity it had displayed in former days, but it continued to function on several levels. Hermann Cohen (1842-1918) in Germany, and Kaufmann Kohler (1843-1926) and Solomon Schechter (1847-1915), who though German-trained, worked in the United States, and a number of other scholars presented the philosophical and theological aspects of Judaism. Some of their younger contemporaries in western Europe followed a somewhat different line of thought, presenting Judaism in terms of personal religious experience. Each of the following four in his own way left an extraordinary impression on Jewish thought, and their biographies deserve consideration as types of Jewish search for religious truth: Claude J. G. Montefiore (1858-1938), Leo Baeck (1873-1956), Franz Rosenzweig (1886-1929), and Martin Buber (1878-   ). Quite apart from their efforts to interpret Judaism, the one thing that all of these had in common was an awareness of the pressing need to redefine in spiritual (as distinguished from historical) terms, the relationship between Judaism and Christianity.

At the beginning of the century, however, such studies were less prominent than the historical. As a pre-eminently history-conscious people, the Jews were more given to the study of the interplay between religion and the conditions of life than to theology, which is by its very nature static. Between the death of Heinrich Graetz (1891), who had seen Jewish history in terms of religious loyalty and rationalistic thought, and that of Simon Dubnow (1942), who described it in terms of culture and community, an incredible amount of research was done into every aspect of the Jewish past. The scientific study of Jewish history (*die Wissenschaft des Judentums*) was carried on with fervor at the seminaries in Europe and by means of numerous monographs and a number of highly scholarly periodicals. In the early part of the twentieth century, similar activity began in the United States. The founding of Dropsie College for Hebrew and Cognate Learning, in Philadelphia in 1907, showed that far-sighted American Jews recognized the importance of such studies. After World War I, a considerable number of the younger European Jewish scholars transferred their activity to America. They prepared the way for the transfer, in the 1930's, of their contemporaries who had stayed behind. Now Palestine and America took over the tasks of Jewish scholarship.

The most effective method by which such scholarly activity was transmuted into guidance for the average person was preaching and instruction by the rabbis. The rabbinate as an institution underwent considerable change as a result of its contacts with western culture. The most obvious of these changes was the growing emphasis on preaching. The rabbi's position was no longer described as "the rabbinical chair," but as "the pulpit." On the other hand, the rabbi never quite abandoned his traditional Jewish duty of teaching, an activity in which he became increasingly involved. Whether through preaching or teaching, the synagogue became the forum where the rabbi presented his views, in the light of Jewish thought and experience, on the problems of Jewish life, and frequently, also on their philosophical backgrounds. The rationalistic emphasis characteristic of the early years of this period, which was followed by the historical, showed signs, after World War II, of giving way to the theological.

The changing religious emphases were, on the whole, too theoretical to have an immediate and direct influence on American Judaism. The exigencies of the Jewish and American situations in the second quarter of the twentieth century called for practical programs rather than theological discussions. Reform rabbis, meeting at Columbus, Ohio, in 1937, effected basic modifications in the radical Pittsburgh Platform of 1885. Among these was a positive attitude towards Zionism and a return—hesitant, to be sure—to broad traditionalism. A rather small minority of these rabbis and their lay followers refused to go along with these changes in the philosophy of Reform Judaism, but this minority never went so far as to secede from the Union of American Hebrew Congregations. At about the same time, Reconstructionism emerged out of the Conservative Jewish movement. Eager to give Jewish life philosophical direction in contemporary terms, Professor Mordecai M. Kaplan defined Judaism as a "religious civilization" that adhered to the Jewish historical view of life, expressed itself in accord with Jewish tradition—though not unmodified—and sought to revive cohesive Jewish community living. Milton Steinberg (1903-1950), a pupil and admirer of Kaplan, was more distinctly theological in his approach. He described Judaism less in pragmatic sociological terms than in intellectual ones in which man accepted the challenges of faith and of history and made conscious efforts to live up to them. At the same time, Will Herberg, deeply affected by the prevailing currents of religious thought, discussed Judaism on an existentialist basis. Others within Conservative Judaism, however, were less eager to find a common philosophical platform than to continue adhering to their basic tenet of continuous adaptation without breaking away from the sources of Jewish tradition. Nor was Orthodox Judaism, though presumably at one on the principle of unchanging tradition, completely united in the face of the cultural differences among its adherents.

All these trends within western Judaism were alike affected by the revival of mystical religion in the western world in the forties and fifties of the century. Among Jews, this took the form of a renaissance of the ideological and theological aspect of Hasidism: recalling that movement's penetrating insights into Judaism and life in general, its religious fervor, and its super-worldliness as distinguished from other-worldliness. The name with which this revival is chiefly connected is Martin Buber; Buber had begun his activity in Germany after World War I, and in the thirties, had gone to Palestine. The wide popularity of the neo-Hasidic attitude among rabbis, teachers, and intellectuals, may be further proof of the hunger for a deeper religious spirit. The chief interpreter of this attitude in the United States has been Abraham J. Heschel, who has exerted wide influence through a series of profound and moving monographs.

Hasidism and Orthodoxy of a different, more personal, type entered the Judaism of the west with the migration from eastern Europe of rabbis, *yeshiva* students, and adherents of a number of Hasidic leaders. These types of Judaism had continued to flourish in that part of the world down to the time of its disintegration under the blows of communism and the horrors of Nazism. The influence of Rabbi Israel Meir Kagan (the *Hafetz Hayyim*, 1838-1933) on the one hand and of the Lubavitcher dynasty of Hasidim on the other—to cite but one example of each type—had been tremendous and widespread. The horrors the Jews were made to suffer during the fourth and fifth decades of the century intensified their religious loyalties. When these groups of undeviatingly Orthodox Jews arrived in the United States —or in Israel—they served as a nucleus around which clustered many Jews of an earlier immigration. They established schools, *yeshivot,* and synagogues of their own. On the whole, this attempt to transplant the east European habits of life into American soil is reminiscent of similar efforts made by immigrants at the beginning of the period under review. Like the earlier attempts, the current one has served to strengthen the totality of Jewish religious life.

Clearly the religious situation among the Jews of America, or almost anywhere else in the diaspora, has become more crystallized, but in variety rather than in unity. Those who still look forward to religious unity as an ideal have therefore turned hopefully to Israel, recalling the prophetic promise that "Out of Zion shall go forth the Law and the word of the Lord from Jerusalem." A proposal to this effect was in fact made and seriously discussed in the middle 1950's. It suggested the convocation of a *synhedrin* that, meeting in the Holy Land, would undertake to legislate on matters of Judaism for Jews everywhere. The idea, however, received a mixed reception both in Israel and the diaspora. For who would be invited to such an assembly, in view of Orthodox Judaism's insistence that it alone can interpret Jewish tradition?

Moreover, the Jews of Israel proved to be at least as far apart in matters of religion as the Jews of the diaspora. The cleavage was brought to the fore when, in 1958, Israel was confronted with the problem of defining the term "Jew." It began as a purely administrative question of how a person was to be identified on his passport. Those who considered Israel a purely secular state gave a secular answer: anyone claiming to be a Jew, or if a minor, having such a claim made for him by his parents, could be so characterized. The rabbinate of Israel, being unexceptionably Orthodox, took issue with such a definition and insisted that to be called a Jew, a person must possess religious qualifications enabling him to belong to the religious community. A similar difference of opinion could not possibly have arisen in the diaspora, where anyone calling himself a Jew is presumed to have certain religious preferences, although he might follow no religious practices and undertake no religious commitments. It is not surprising that important Jewish scholars in the diaspora, to whom Ben-Gurion unofficially submitted this problem of definition, replied with practical unanimity that the term "Jew" had religious connotations.

It was, moreover, only natural for the interpretations and viewpoints developed in the diaspora to seek an opportunity for expression in Israel. The Conservative and Reform organizations in the United States sought recognition in Israel as legitimate manifestations of Judaism. But the rabbinate of Israel refused to accede to any such demand, on the ground that both these American religious organizations had, to a greater or lesser extent, broken with talmudic law. At the same time, the government of Israel was bound to permit both Reform and Conservative Judaism to establish institutions through which each hopes to clarify its stand. A generation will probably have to pass before it becomes clear to what extent either viewpoint will appeal to Israel's youth. Certainly whatever modification of religious law and observance takes place in Israel will be indigenous to that state and answerable to its own cultural and religious needs.

4. EDUCATION FOR YOUNG AND OLD

The efforts to restore meaning and reawaken loyalty to Jewish life have been seriously impeded in the American environment by an inability to solve the problems of Jewish education. Serious attempts to increase the content and improve the methods of Jewish education, which had begun in the second decade of the twentieth century, gained momentum in the succeeding years. Schools for the training of American-born teachers were opened in a number of cities. Gratz College, established in 1897 in Philadelphia, was the first of its kind; the Teachers Institute of the Jewish Theological Seminary (1909), in New York, was the second. Thereafter, similar schools were established in Chicago, Baltimore, Boston, and other large cities, and several others were established in New York City. The graduates of these schools joined the devoted and learned teachers who had come from Europe after World War I, so that the newer type of Jewish teacher deservedly gained in professional status. A new spirit now permeated the Jewish religious school, where Hebrew began to be taught as a living language, and Jewish ceremonials as living, meaningful, vibrant traditions. Moreover, although the *Kehilla* movement did not survive, community interest in education, which the *Kehilla* had awakened, did continue. Jewish community organizations, now to be found in almost every city and town, though primarily philanthropic and defensive in their motivation, assumed greater educational responsibility. Many of the larger cities established central bureaus of Jewish education, with trained pedagogues heading them and on their staffs. The American Association for Jewish Education, organized in 1939, consists of laymen who seek to stimulate and guide Jewish education throughout the United States.

In the more recent decades, the trend has been away from the communal school and toward the synagogue school. In his effort to bring more order into American Jewish life at the beginning of the century, Dr. Solomon Schechter had laid it down as a rule that a synagogue must conduct an elementary Jewish school as part of its congregational functions. The graduates of the Jewish Theological Seminary took this advice to heart and established synagogue schools for the children of the members. A little later, the rabbis trained at the Rabbi Isaac Elhanan Theological Seminary (Yeshiva) adopted the same policy. As synagogue affiliation increased, the number of children attending community schools began to fall off. This trend may have been, as some claim, due to the fact that more parents, under the influence of the rabbi, were persuaded to provide their children with a better grounding in their heritage. But because many such parents were evidently not persuaded to subordinate their children's other physical and cultural interests, the number of sessions in the afternoon Jewish schools had to be reduced, so that their general pattern called for a maximum of some seven hours per week as against the minimum of ten to fifteen hours that was formerly the rule. To make up for this loss of time and other difficulties, reliance has been placed on improvement of the curriculum.

Far more hopeful developments, however, have taken place in several other areas of Jewish educational effort. There has been a substantial growth in postelementary Jewish education for children of high-school age, and successful experiments have been conducted with a few summer camps where Hebrew speech and religious instruction are part of the program. Moreover, an institution quite unlooked for a generation ago has come into being: the all-day Jewish school with a more or less integrated program of Jewish and general subjects. The new Hasidic communities have been most active in this type of school, and their success has encouraged others to try the like. In 1958 there were more than 214 such schools, mostly under noncongregational auspices, throughout the United States, 136 of them in New York City. The total number is one per cent of all the nonpublic schools run by private and denominational organizations in the country. The results of a survey made by the American Association for Jewish Education, issued in 1959, indicate that over 550,000 children enroll annually in the various types of Jewish school, but that almost half of this number attend but one day a week, Sunday morning.

The idea of integrating the two cultural areas in which the American Jew must live spread into adult education. Discussions on the desirability of a Jewish-sponsored university had begun in the 1920's and gained momentum during the years when colleges and professional, especially medical, schools discriminated against Jewish applicants for admission. The plan was finally implemented when, as a result of the initiative of Dr. Israel Goldstein, Brandeis University opened its doors in the fall of 1948, under the presidency of Abram L. Sachar, as a nonsectarian collegiate institution with a well-staffed department of Jewish studies as part of the usual college course. Even earlier—as early as 1928—the Rabbi Isaac Elhanan Theological Seminary opened an undergraduate collegiate department. Before long, it accepted nontheological students as well; eventually it added graduate courses. It thereupon changed its name to Yeshiva University. Even a medical school is now part of Yeshiva University.

Other cultural institutions have made similar efforts to strengthen their foundations and broaden their influence. The Jewish Theological Seminary opened the University of Judaism, a branch in Los Angeles, that has the right to grant graduate degrees in the field of Jewish studies. The Hebrew Union College of Cincinnati and the Jewish Institute of Religion in New York (founded by Stephen S. Wise in 1922) joined forces, and both institutions function under the same directorate. The Hebrew Union College also opened a school in Los Angeles.

One of the astonishing manifestations of current Jewish life has been the vitality of the Yiddish language and culture. Yiddish speech, to be sure, no longer dominates the Jewish neighborhoods. The number of Yiddish newspaper readers has dwindled, as was to have been expected. Yet the use of the language has remained considerable and the variety, volume, and quality of its literature exceptionally high. If the characteristic note of this literature has become one of nostalgia, it can be easily explained as the result of an overwhelming desire to keep alive the beautiful memories of a civilization in which the authors as well as the culture grew to maturity. Yiddishist organizations have at great sacrifice maintained schools for elementary school and high school children; the Yiddish language and literature are the main subjects of instruction. The above-mentioned survey made by the American Association of Jewish Education indicates that the total annual enrollment in these schools throughout the country is about 10,000. Yiddish studies have been introduced into the curriculums of several universities in New York; a chair in Yiddish language and literature has been established in the Hebrew University in Jerusalem.

An example of an influential cultural institution among the Jews of both North and South America is the Yivo Institute for Jewish Research. Organized in Vilna, the old "Jerusalem of Lithuania," in 1925, to promote historical and sociological research, it was compelled in 1929 to transfer all its activities to the Western Hemisphere; its headquarters are in New York. Its monthly in Yiddish, its annual volume of studies in Yiddish and English, its monographs, and its valuable library and archives testify to great earnestness and high achievement.

The transformation in the elementary educational picture in the past forty years has been paralleled, though not equalled, by changes in the field of adult education. Every organized Jewish group has adopted an educational program. Synagogues, centers, B'nai B'rith lodges, Zionist and other groups maintain programs of lectures and study circles; and the National Jewish Welfare Board, the National Association of Jewish Community Centers, maintains a lecture bureau and other services for the enrichment of Jewish programs. Even if the motivation for these activities is frequently social, their popularity bespeaks a revival of a traditional Jewish approach to life. Such study, it must be admitted, is largely on a popular, elementary level. But at least, the problem presented by intellectual poverty is recognized, and the will to solve it is there.

Whether in English, Hebrew, or Yiddish, on the adult or the juvenile level, in fiction or works of scholarship, recent literary activity among Jews has been significant. The Jewish Publication Society is no longer the only publisher of books of history and fiction on Jewish subjects; commercial publishers and even university presses have discovered that an interested Jewish reading public exists. The day is past when Jewish scholarship has to subsist on borrowings from Europe. There is, to be sure, much that can be criticized; weaknesses and inadequacies are apparent in every area of

Jewish culture and religion; there is still a wide chasm between reality and what might have been expected in spiritual and intellectual productivity from a Jewish community so fortunately placed.

The all-important question is whether the Jewish community as a whole can be awakened in time to meet its cultural responsibilities. Evidence of improvement in the outlook of the American Jew can be seen in the establishment of the National Foundation for Jewish Culture. Some of the most prominent leaders of the Jewish communities in the United States, meeting in 1960 in the annual assembly of the Council of Jewish Federations and Welfare Funds, brought the new foundation into being. It was assigned the tasks of assisting cultural institutions already in existence and of stimulating the development of new facets of Jewish cultural activity. It remains to be seen whether those who voted for the establishment of the foundation will provide it with the means to realize these objectives. The American Jew's response to this effort will be an index of the cultural maturity of Jewish leadership in the United States.

VII

. . . .

The Balance Sheet of a Generation

. . . .

The last few years of the period here under discussion have seen several important anniversary celebrations. In 1954 and 1955 the Jewish community of the United States observed the tercentenary of its origin. In 1955 and 1956 the Jewish community of Great Britain observed a similar anniversary. Comparisons and contrasts between their small and uncertain beginnings and the present size and strength of these two western communities were inevitable. Both communities, however, as well as the Jews of the rest of the world, had undergone more radical transformations in the previous sixty or seventy years than in the entire previous millennium. Few periods in the long history of the Jews had been as revolutionary, as tragic, and as inspiring. The problems and the difficulties had been of such magnitude as to justify the view that the mere survival of an identifiable Jewish group might well have been miraculous. Yet the Jewish people not only survived, but also displayed such constructive spiritual powers as to enable it to add an interesting, and in some particulars, a thrilling chapter to Jewish history.

An important part of such a chapter is represented by another anniversary observed in these recent years—the tenth anniversary of Israel's statehood. The very existence of Israel, brought into being and maintained in the face of great odds, testifies to the vitality of the Jewish people. And the state has achieved much more than independence. With Hebrew dominating its daily life, Israel has deepened Jewish culture, education, and religion. It has absorbed almost a million newcomers whom it has caused to strike root in the land sacred to their fathers. It has shown wisdom in government and restraint in the face of provocation. Confronted with innumerable problems, it has striven for peace, unity, and social betterment. At the end of its tenth year, Israel stood forth as a spiritual and political achievement without parallel. Curiously enough, it is one of the few spots on this troubled earth where men look to the future with confident optimism.

This most recent period of Jewish history can be summarized on two different levels, and thus two different conclusions can be drawn from it. It can be argued that the Jews have been nothing more than victims of historical forces: their migrations, the result of politics and prejudice; their adjustments to new environments, but individual successes; their community organizations, mere manifestations of minority reactions to pressure by the majority; and even the establishment of Israel, an accidental outcome of international rivalries. A case can be, and has been, made for such a view. It is the view of those who see the Jewish people with the jaundiced eye of the anti-Semite or of the alienated Jew, or of those who smugly explain Jewish survival either by the Ahasuerus legend or in the more intellectualized terminology of "fossil civilization." According to such views, there is neither sense nor purpose in remaining a Jew; to do so is a manifestation of stubbornness, or worse still, of racial narcissism.

The trouble with such explanations is that, by ignorance or design, they do not explain. Mere stubbornness or self-adulation could not have persisted in the face of terror and martyrdom; above all, these barren attitudes could not have led to spiritual productivity. No people—not even a powerful nation—can be said to be living or dead because it dominates or fails to dominate historical forces. Such domination occurs too rarely, if at all, to be considered a realistic test. A better test of a people's vitality is its ability to stand up to historical forces and to try to be true to its values no matter how much or how suddenly conditions vary. By this test, the Jewish people has been very much alive during the sixty years just past. All one need do is consider some of the events mentioned above. Those Jews who emigrated from eastern Europe, for example, did so in large part for economic reasons; but they could have remained at home and improved their social and economic status by losing themselves in the majority. Their religion and culture must have, to put it mildly, meant something to them if it played so important a part in so momentous a decision. And the very many more Jews who did not emigrate, if one is to judge them by the personalities they produced and the broad human ideas that came from among them, were certainly not a dull and inert mass of humanity. Nor could it have been sheer accident that so many of the adjustments that so many immigrants made in their new homes were so frequently related to, and in harmony with, the intellectual and spiritual values of traditional Jewish life. The sense of mutual brotherly responsibility that created effective philanthropic institutions, both local and world-wide; the unquenchable hope for restoration to free life in the Holy Land which developed a community prepared to assert its claims to self-expression; the literary achievements in every language and the creation of literatures in two languages that were themselves the creations of the Jewish spirit; the social and educational institutions to fill every cultural, religious, and philosophical need; even the fervid religious disputations and disagreements within the Jewish community —all of these and more are irrefutable proofs that Judaism is a functioning religion and culture with a great deal to offer to its adherents and to mankind as a whole.

These, it should be noted, were achievements of the Jewish people in an age and under conditions of personal and cultural freedom, especially in the west, but in eastern Europe as well. The Jewish spirit had also functioned in previous eras and under less auspicious circumstances, but at a much slower tempo and with less variety of expression. The greater needs and challenges of the present day have produced and are producing more diversified and more numerous responses. Moreover, because the Jewish spirit functions in close contact with different peoples and cultures, Jewish responses can frequently benefit the wider community. In this sense one can talk of Jewish contributions to civilization: in the labor movement, in philanthropy, in social work, in such political inventions as the Minority Treaties, and even in religion when Judaism has been articulate in the presentation of its own point of view. This enumeration naturally takes no account of the individual Jew's activity in the life of the nation of which he is a citizen. The fact that Jews have been and are more prominent in some areas of life than in others may derive from Jewish fate and tradition, but it would take considerable psychological and statistical investigation to prove this. One can only hope that the Jew's Jewishness will continue to mold him into a socially valuable personality as it has, without doubt, made him a member in a socially valuable group.

Such a future is, however, by no means certain. The very survival of the Jewish diaspora has been doubted. The number of those losing contact with Jewish values and severing their connections with the Jewish community has been on the increase all through the past century. This and the falling birth rate among the Jews of the diaspora will, at best, probably keep the world's Jewish population merely stationary. What is more, there is every indication that unless there is a change for the better in Russia—which is of course not impossible—the estimated 2,500,000 Jews of the Soviet Union must also be written off. This loss would mean that within one generation the Jewish population of the world would have been reduced by almost half. Pessimists, sociologists, and Jewish nationalists—a strange combination —argue that environmental pressures are bound to eliminate the diaspora entirely. Pressures of various kinds give no promise of abating in the most populous diaspora community, that of the United States. There is no reason to assume that these and other forces will cease in the foreseeable future to weaken those Jews who are ill-equipped to withstand them.

Herein, therefore, lies the foremost task for the future of diaspora Judaism. It may yet turn out that of all the costly activities and great institutions created by this generation to meet the problems of our day, those who retain Jewish awareness in the next generation will be most grateful for the seemingly minor and comparatively inexpensive efforts to establish and maintain the all-day school and the Hebrew summer camps for children, and for the study circles and institutes and Jewish college courses for adults. For, in the final analysis, the sources of Jewish vitality have always been the literature and the ceremonial and religious teachings that mold the Jewish personality. The generation just past was able to answer the challenges hurled at it because it was not too far removed from that cultural-religious complex which goes by the name of Judaism. Even a casual view of the Jewish scene reveals that the further removed any group of Jews has been from this source of Jewish life, the weaker have been its Jewish responses. Our generation, therefore, will inevitably be judged by its success or failure in transmitting these ideas and attitudes as functioning realities. Judaism warns against relying on miracles; one may pray and hope for them, but not sit back and depend on their coming to pass. It will be a miracle if a Jewish people survives two or three more generations—unless the Jews of the present day take steps to stem the increasing alienation from the sources of Jewish life. Only if the current revival of interest in religion—or in the intellectualized aspects of Jewish life that go by the name of Jewish culture —is expressed in a meaningful and plentiful Jewish education, will one be able to look hopefully to the future.

But intellect, leadership, and organizational forms will have to undergo radical changes if any such intensified training in Jewishness is to become the rule. Jewish life will have to assume more meaning than merely another expression of man's need to worship. Leadership, both lay and professional, will have to be judged by more than energy, organizing ability, and a social outlook. It will have to understand and react to the problem of transmitting Jewish knowledge and values. The entire community will have to reorganize in terms of a changed focus, away from the centrality of defense and philanthropy. There is practically no evidence at the moment that any such revolutionary changes in leadership and purpose, on any considerable scale, are in the offing in any diaspora community. There are only scattered individuals and a few comparatively small groups—with little influence on the so-called top leadership—who are deeply enough concerned about maximum Jewish living. Therefore, from this viewpoint too, the outlook is for a Jewish community considerably reduced in size and tragically lacking in spirit.

Perhaps what is most needed is leadership with ability, devotion, and prestige, to give voice and direction to the inner strivings of Jewish life. Such leadership has, in fact, in various times of need, arisen in the past. For the present, and for the immediate future, one may look to influences likely to come from Israel. The diaspora cannot afford to consider the new State as merely a political entity that has already realized the hope of restoration. Unless Torah comes out of Zion, it will not have fulfilled Jewish aspirations. Israel need not become a theocratic state, and it probably will not; but it must exert cultural and religious influences on diaspora life, as the Jewish community of Palestine did in the distant past. Under these conditions, the diaspora's contacts with Israel are of the utmost importance. Quite apart from supporting Israel materially, as the diaspora will have to continue doing for a long time, it will also have to foster Israel's cultural and religious institutions with unabated vigor.

But while aware of all the dangers inherent in their current situation, the Jews have no reason for despair. Awareness is, indeed, sure to take the Jewish people a considerable way toward the solution of the problems that threaten its future. We must at all times realize that the maintenance of our essential difference in a free society cannot be easy. Life in an environment that permits cultural give and take is bound to be hazardous for a minority. But the past two generations, like other periods in Jewish history, have demonstrated the possibility of attaining an integrated personality in which Judaism and western culture fuse harmoniously and creatively. There must be faith that the process will continue in the generations to come. If prejudices of various intensities do not intervene, the process will be a happier one than in the half century just past. If the Jews are more careful to balance their general culture with a more ample supply of Jewish knowledge, experience, and spirituality, the results will be of even greater value to civilization. In any event, the continuance of Judaism and of the Jewish people need not be questioned: Jewish experience in the recent past gives high promise of a brighter future.

Bibliography

From the limited number of titles listed below, it is obvious that no attempt has been made to offer anything even approaching an exhaustive bibliography. The sole aim has been to provide the interested reader with material for a further investigation of various important facets of Jewish life during the period covered by this book.

Much of the material on which the above discussion is based can be found in current periodicals: *Commentary*, and its predecessor, *The Contemporary Jewish Record*, *Congress Bi-Weekly* (until recently a weekly), *The Jewish Frontier*, *Midstream*, *Judaism*, *The Reconstructionist*. These and some others usually present informed opinion. In addition, there are valuable publications that contain historical and sociological analyses: *American Jewish Archives*, a semiannual established in June 1948; *Publications of the American Jewish Historical Society*, a quarterly since its 39th volume in September 1949; *Jewish Social Studies*, a quarterly since 1939; *The YIVO Annual of Jewish Social Science*, since 1946. Most useful as a work of reference and for reconstructing the trends of the entire period has been the *American Jewish Year Book*, the first volume of which appeared in 1899.

GENERAL WORKS

ELBOGEN, ISMAR. *A Century of Jewish Life, 1840-1940*. Philadelphia: Jewish Publication Society, 1944.

GRAYZEL, SOLOMON. *A History of the Jews*. Philadelphia: Jewish Publication Society, 1947, 1952.

LEARSI, RUFUS. *Israel: A History of the Jewish People.* New York: The World Publishing Co., 1949.

MARGOLIS, MAX L., and MARX, ALEXANDER. *A History of the Jewish People.* Philadelphia: Jewish Publication Society, 1927.

MENES, A., and others, eds. *The Jewish People, Past and Present.* (A collection of scholarly essays), 4 vols. New York: Central Yiddish Culture Organization (CYCO), 1946-1955.

ROTH, CECIL. *A Short History of the Jewish People.* London: East and West Library, 1936, 1959.

SACHAR, ABRAM L. *Sufferance Is the Badge: The Jew in the Contemporary World.* New York: Alfred A. Knopf, 1940.

SACHAR, HOWARD M. *The Course of Modern Jewish History.* New York: The World Publishing Co., 1958.

AMERICAN EXPERIENCE

BENTWICH, NORMAN. *For Zion's Sake: A Biography of Judah L. Magnes.* Philadelphia: Jewish Publication Society, 1954.

——*Solomon Schechter: A Biography.* Philadelphia: Jewish Publication Society, 1940.

DAVIDSON, GABRIEL. *Our Jewish Farmers and the Story of the Jewish Agricultural Society.* New York: L. B. Fischer Publishing Co., 1943.

DUSHKIN, ALEXANDER M., and ENGELMAN, URIAH Z. *Report of the Commission for the Study of Jewish Education in the United States,* vol. I (1959). New York: American Assn. for Jewish Education.

EPSTEIN, MELECH. *Jewish Labor in the U.S.A.,* vol. I, 1882-1914; vol. II, 1914-1952. New York: Trade Union Sponsoring Committee, 1950, 1953.

FOSTER, ARNOLD, and EPSTEIN, BENJAMIN. *Cross-Currents* (report of the Anti-Defamation League of B'nai B'rith). New York: Doubleday and Co., 1956.

GINZBERG, ELI. *Report to American Jews on Overseas Relief, Palestine and Refugees in the United States.* New York: Harper and Bros., 1942.

GLAZER, NATHAN. "Social Characteristics of American Jews, 1654-1954." In *American Jewish Year Book,* vol. LVI (1955), pp. 3-41. Philadelphia: Jewish Publication Society.

GOLDBERG, NATHAN. "Dynamics of the Economic Structure of the Jews in the United States." In *Publications of AJHS*, vol. VLVI, no. 3 (March 1957), pp. 233 ff. New York: American Jewish Historical Society.

HANDLIN, OSCAR. *Adventure in Freedom: Three Hundred Years of Jewish Life in America*. New York: McGraw-Hill Book Co., 1954.

——and MARY F. "The Acquisition of Political and Social Rights by the Jews in the United States." In *American Jewish Year Book*, vol. LVI (1955), pp. 43-98. Philadelphia: Jewish Publication Society.

HERBERG, WILL. "The Jewish Labor Movement in the United States," In *American Jewish Year Book*, vol. LIII (1952). Philadelphia: Jewish Publication Society.

HIGHAM, JOHN. *Strangers in the Land: Patterns of American Nativism, 1860-1925*. New Brunswick, N.J.: Rutgers University Press, 1955.

JANOWSKY, OSCAR I., ed. *The American Jew: A Composite Portrait*. New York: Harper and Bros., 1942.

JOSEPH, SAMUEL. *History of the Baron de Hirsch Fund: The Americanization of the Jewish Immigrant*. New York: Baron de Hirsch Fund, 1935.

——*Jewish Immigration to the United States, 1881-1910*. New York: Columbia University, 1914.

LEARSI, RUFUS. *The Jews in America: A History*. New York: The World Publishing Co., 1954.

LEWISOHN, LUDWIG. *The American Jew: Character and Destiny*. New York: Farrar, Straus and Cudahy, 1950.

MIHANOVICH, CLEMENT S. "The American Immigration Policy." In *Publications of AJHS*, vol. XLVI, no. 3 (March 1957), pp. 306 ff. New York: American Jewish Historical Society.

RABINOWITZ, BENJAMIN. "A History of the YMHA." In *Publications of AJHS*, vol. XXXVII (1948). New York: American Jewish Historical Society.

REZNIKOFF, CHARLES, ed. *Louis Marshall, Champion of Liberty*, 2 vols. Philadelphia: Jewish Publication Society, 1957.

SCHACHNER, NATHAN. *The Price of Liberty: A History of the American Jewish Committee*. New York: The American Jewish Committee, 1948.

SKLAR, MARSHALL, ed. *The Jews: Social Patterns of an American Group.* Glencoe, Ill.: The Free Press, 1958.

SOLOMON, BARBARA MILLER. *Ancestors and Immigrants: A Changing New England Tradition.* Cambridge, Mass.: Harvard University Press, 1956.

STEIN, HERMAN D. "Jewish Social Work in the United States." In *American Jewish Year Book,* vol. LVII (1956), pp. 3-98. Philadelphia: Jewish Publication Society.

WEINRYB, BERNARD D. "Jewish Immigration and Accommodation to America: Research, Facts, Problems." In *Publications of AJHS,* vol. XLVI, no. 3 (March 1957), pp. 366-403. New York: American Jewish Historical Society.

WISCHNITZER, MARK. *To Dwell in Safety: The Story of Jewish Migration since 1800.* Philadelphia: Jewish Publication Society, 1948.

——*Visas to Freedom: the History of HIAS.* New York: World Publishing Co., 1956.

EUROPEAN EXPERIENCE

CLAUDE, INIS L., JR. *National Minorities: An International Problem.* Cambridge, Mass.: Harvard University Press, 1955.

FREEDMAN, MAURICE, ed. *A Minority in Britain: Social Studies of the Anglo-Jewish Community.* London: Vallentine, Mitchell and Co., 1955.

FRIEDMAN, PHILIP. *Martyrs and Fighters: An Epic of the Warsaw Ghetto.* New York: Frederick A. Praeger, 1954.

——*Their Brother's Keepers* (Christians who protected Jews during the Nazi occupation). New York: Crown Publishers, 1957.

GROSSMAN, KURT R. *Germany's Moral Debt: The German-Israel Agreement.* Washington, D.C.: Public Affairs Press, 1954.

JANOWSKY, OSCAR I. *Nationalities and National Minorities.* New York: Macmillan Co., 1945.

LEO BAECK. *Institute Annual,* essays in the history of the Jews in Germany, 1956, 1957, 1958. London: East and West Library.

LIPMAN, V. D. *Social History of the Jews in England, 1850-1950.* London: Watts and Co., 1954.

MARCUS, JACOB R. *Rise and Destiny of the German Jew*. Cincinnati, O.: Union of American Hebrew Congregations, 1934.

MEYER, PETER, and others. *The Jews in the Soviet Satellites*. Syracuse, N.Y.: Syracuse University Press (for the American Jewish Committee), 1953.

POLIAKOV, LEON. *Harvest of Hate: The Nazi Program for the Destruction of the Jews of Europe*. Philadelphia: Jewish Publication Society, 1954.

RINGELBLUM, EMMANUEL. *Notes from the Warsaw Ghetto*, translated and edited by Jacob Sloan. New York: McGraw-Hill, 1958.

ROBINSON, JACOB, and others. *Were the Minorities Treaties a Failure?* New York: Institute of Jewish Affairs of World Jewish Congress, 1943.

ROBINSON, NEHEMIAH, ed. *European Jewry Ten Years After the War*. New York: Institute of Jewish Affairs of World Jewish Congress, 1956.

SCHWARZ, LEO W. *The Redeemers: a Saga of the Years 1945-1952*. New York: Farrar, Straus and Young, 1953.

SCHWARZ, SOLOMON M. *The Jews in the Soviet Union*. Syracuse, N.Y.: Syracuse University Press (for the American Jewish Committee), 1951.

TARTAKOVER, ARIEH, and GROSSMAN, KURT R. *The Jewish Refugee*. New York: Institute of Jewish Affairs of World Jewish Congress, 1944.

TEMKIN, S. D. "Three Centuries of Jewish Life in England." In *American Jewish Year Book*, vol. LVIII (1957), pp. 3-63. Philadelphia: Jewish Publication Society.

MORE DISTANT DIASPORAS

LANDSHUT, S. *Jewish Communities in the Muslim Countries of the Middle East: A Survey*. London: the Jewish Chronicle, 1950.

RESNER, LAWRENCE. *Eternal Stranger: The Plight of the Modern Jew from Baghdad to Casablanca*. New York: Doubleday, 1951.

SARON, GUSTAV, and HOTZ, LOUIS, eds. *The Jews in South Africa*. London: Oxford University Press, 1955.

ZIONISM AND NATIONALIST THEORIES

BEIN, ALEX. *Theodore Herzl: A Biography.* Philadelphia: Jewish Publication Society, 1941, 1956.

BEN HORIN, MEIR. *Max Nordau: Philosopher of Human Solidarity.* New York: Conference of Jewish Social Studies, 1957.

BERLIN, ISAIAH. *Chaim Weizmann.* New York: Farrar, Straus and Cudahy, 1958.

HERTZBERG, ARTHUR J. *The Zionist Idea.* New York: Doubleday and The Herzl Press, 1959.

LEARSI, RUFUS. *Fulfillment: The Epic Story of Zionism.* New York: World Publishing Co., 1951.

LIPSKY, LOUIS. *A Gallery of Zionist Profiles.* New York: Farrar, Straus and Cudahy, 1956.

MEYER, ISIDORE, ed. *Early History of Zionism in America.* New York: American Jewish Historical Society and The Herzl Foundation, 1958.

PATAI, RAPHAEL, ed. *Herzl Year Book,* vol. I (1958), vol. II (1959). New York: The Herzl Press.

PINSON, KOPPEL S., ed. *Simon Dubnow, Nationalism and History.* Philadelphia: Jewish Publication Society, 1958.

RABINOWICZ, OSKAR K. *Herzl, Architect of the Balfour Declaration.* New York: The Herzl Institute (pamphlet), 1958.

SIMON, LEON. *Ahad Ha'Am: A Biography.* Philadelphia: Jewish Publication Society, 1960.

WEIZMANN, CHAIM. *Trial and Error: An Autobiography.* Philadelphia: Jewish Publication Society, 1949.

ISRAEL

BERNSTEIN, MARVER H. *The Politics of Israel: The First Decade of Statehood.* Princeton, N.J.: Princeton University Press, 1957.

DAVIS, MOSHE, ed. *Israel: Its Role in Civilization.* New York: Harper and Bros., 1956.

FRANK, WALDO D. *Bridgehead: The Drama of Israel.* New York: Braziller, 1957.

Israel and the United Nations. New York: Manhattan Publishing Co. (for the Carnegie Foundation of International Peace), 1957.

JANOWSKY, OSCAR I. *Foundations of Israel: Emergence of a Welfare State.* New York: Van Nostrand (an Anvil original), 1959.

LEVENSOHN, LOTTA. *Vision and Fulfillment: The First 25 Years of the Hebrew University, 1925-1950.* New York: The Greystone Press, 1950.

MARSHALL, SAMUEL L. A. *Sinai Victory.* New York: Morrow, 1958.

PATAI, RAPHAEL. *Israel Between East and West: A Study in Human Relations.* Philadelphia: Jewish Publication Society, 1953.

SHUMSKY, ABRAHAM. *The Clash of Cultures in Israel: A Problem for Education.* New York: Teachers College, Columbia University, 1955.

WILLIAMS, L. F. RUSHBROOK. *The State of Israel.* New York: Macmillan Company, 1957.

EXPRESSION IN LITERATURE

BENSHALOM, BENZION. *Hebrew Literature Between Two World Wars.* Jerusalem: Youth and Hechalutz Dept. of the Zionist Organization (pamphlet), 1953.

FIEDLER, LESLIE A. *The Jew in the American Novel.* New York: The Herzl Institute (pamphlet), 1958.

HALKIN, SIMON. *Modern Hebrew Literature: Trends and Values.* New York: Schocken Books, 1950.

JEWISH BOOK COUNCIL OF AMERICA, *Annual* (since 1942). New York.

LEFTWICH, JOSEPH. *Israel Zangwill.* New York: Yoseloff, 1957.

ROBACK, A. A. *Contemporary Yiddish Literature: A brief outline.* London: World Jewish Congress, British section (Popular Jewish Library), 1957.

SILBERSCHLAG, EISIG. *Hebrew Literature: an Evaluation.* New York: Herzl Institute (pamphlet), 1959.

SPIEGEL, SHALOM. *Hebrew Reborn.* New York: Macmillan Company, 1930.

WALLENROD, REUBEN. *The Literature of Modern Israel.* New York: Abelard-Schuman, 1956.

EXPRESSION IN RELIGION

BLAU, JOSEPH L. "The Spiritual Life of American Jewry, 1654-1954." In *American Jewish Year Book,* vol. LVI (1955), pp. 99-170. Philadelphia: Jewish Publication Society.

BOKSER, BEN-ZION. *Judaism and Modern Man: Essays in Jewish Theology.* New York: Philosophical Library, 1957.

CENTRAL CONFERENCE OF AMERICAN RABBIS. *Year Book,* since 1900. Cincinnati, Ohio: Central Conference of American Rabbis.

COHEN, ARTHUR A. *Anatomy of Faith: Milton Steinberg.* New York: Harcourt, Brace and Co., 1960.

FRIEDMAN, MAURICE S. *Martin Buber: The Life of Dialogue.* Chicago, Ill.: Chicago University Press, 1955.

GLAZER, NATHAN. *American Judaism: An Historical Survey of the Jewish Religion in America.* Chicago, Ill.: The University of Chicago Press, 1957.

KAPLAN, MORDECAI M. *The Future of the American Jew.* New York: Macmillan Company, 1948.

——*Judaism as a Civilization: Toward a Reconstruction of American Jewish Life,* 2nd edition. New York: The Reconstructionist Press, 1957.

RABBINICAL ASSEMBLY OF AMERICA. *Proceedings* (of annual meetings), since 1936. New York: Rabbinical Assembly.

ROTHSCHILD, FRITZ. *Between God and Man* (an exposition of the thought of A. J. Heschel). New York: Harper and Bros., 1959.

SKLARE, MARSHALL. *Conservative Judaism: An American Religious Movement.* Glencoe, Ill.: The Free Press, 1955.

WAXMAN, MORDECAI, ed. *Tradition and Change: The Development of Conservative Judaism.* New York: Burning Bush Press, 1958.

Index

SOLOMON GRAYZEL was graduated as a rabbi from the Jewish Theological Seminary and received a Ph.D. in history from Dropsie College for Hebrew and Cognate Learning. For eighteen years he taught Jewish history at Gratz College in Philadelphia. He is the author of *The Church and the Jews in the Thirteenth Century* (1933) and of *A History of the Jews* (1947) and a frequent contributor to scholarly and popular publications. In 1957 the National Jewish Welfare Board bestowed on Dr. Grayzel its Frank L. Weil Award for "distinguished contribution to American Jewish culture."